The Non-Trepreneurs

Escaping Corporate Life
For a Life of Financial Freedom

Julie and Jason Buckley

Copyright © Julie and Jason Buckley

First Published: October 2020

Updated: February 2021

This Version: July 2022

Front Cover: The Authors at Erg Chebbi, Morocco

The author has made every effort to ensure the accuracy of the information held within this book. However, much of the information given is personal opinion, and no liability can be accepted for errors contained within.

This book provides general information and not recommendations to act. If you are unsure, please seek independent professional investment advice before entering into any financial transaction. Entering into any financial transaction that involves shares, bonds, property or other investments puts your capital at risk.

Contents

Please Read This First 1

Part One: The Non-Trepreneurs 3

    What is a Non-Trepreneur?   4
    How Do They Do It?   6
    Why Become a Non-Trepreneur?   10
    Who Can Become a Non-Trepreneur?   11
    How Can We Earn Our Freedom?   16
    How Long Does the Path Take?   20
    How Much Money Do You Need   22
    Where Does this Wealth Come From?   23
    What's Wrong with Work?   27
    Our Personal Non-Trepreneur Story   29
    In Summary   39

Part Two: The Freedom Mindset 40

    The Standard Mindset   40
    The Status Mindset   43
    The Money Mindset   45
    The Obstacle Mindset   46
    The Control Mindset   47
    The Retirement Mindset   48
    The Work Mindset   49
    The Relationship Mindset   51
    The Media & News Mindset   52
    The Capability Mindset   53
    The Risk Mindset   54
    In Summary   55

Part Three: Seven Stages to Freedom 57

    Stage 1: Get the Idea   58
    Stage 2: Think Like a Business   58
    Stage 3: Plug the Leaks   68
    Stage 4: Weave a Safety Net   70
    Stage 5: Build Cash Engines   71
    Stage 6: Increasing Your Income   73
    Stage 7: Work Becomes Optional   76
    In Summary   80

Part Four: An Efficiently Spent Life 81

    An Average Financial Life   81
    The Compounding Effect of Saving   83
    The Big Five Costs   86
    A Thousand Cuts from the Smaller Knives   95
    Our Cost Tracking System   97
    Dragged Down by Deprivation?   97
    The More Radical Options   100
    In Summary   103

Part Five: Increasing Income 105

    Continual Education   105
    Doing What Others Won't   106
    Going Self-Employed   107
    Value Yourself   109
    Ready-Made Side Gigs   110
    Earning from Investments   111
    In Summary   111

Part Six: Building Cash Engines 112

    Accidental Investors   113
    Our Non-Trepreneur Investing Principles   114
    The Investments We Use   120
    Other Non-Trepreneur Investments   142

Taxes	144
In Summary	146

Part Seven: Seeking Balance 147

What Makes A Good Life?	147
Comfort & Discomfort	151
Work Life	152
Ownership & Agility	153
Thrift	154
In Summary	155

Part Eight: The Reality of (Very) Early Retirement 157

Stepping into the Blinding Light	157
Shedding Guilt	159
Losing an Identity	161
Bouncing Back into Work	162
The Entrepreneur Opportunity	163
Ongoing Risks	164
Ongoing Wealth Management	165
In Summary	166

Appendix A: Savings Ideas 168

Transport	168
Housing	169
Food	169
Clothing	170
Pets	170
Entertainment	170
Holidays	170
Insurance	171
Technology	171
Taxes	171

Appendix B: Further Support 172
    Books   172
    Websites and Blogs   173
    Podcasts   174
    US Translator   174

About the Authors 176
    A Cheeky Request   176
    Other Books by the Authors   177

Please Read This First

Aged 43, seven years ago, I retired. My wife Julie had already quit work a few months before me, at the same age. Through a combination of accidental and purposeful investing, plus a strong focus on our spending, we engineered a position where working became a choice, rather than a need. All our life expenses are paid by a combination of rental income, share dividends, solar panel payments and bond interest. We have private pensions which will start to bolster this income from age 55 onwards. To stave off boredom and give us a sense of contribution and progression, we travel, write blog posts and books, and complete other small projects, which generate an additional income above our needs.

So, we have first-hand experience of what we're talking about in this book. But it's important to understand that we're both amateur investors. Our backgrounds are in IT and marketing, we're not finance professionals. We have no finance qualifications and nothing we've written in this book should be taken as financial advice. Our approach was to self-educate ourselves about personal finance and investing and, so far, our financial plan has worked well for us. We strongly believe our approach will continue to work in the decades to come, but there are no guarantees.

This is a book written for those like us, who earn good incomes, but aren't fulfilled with the work to earn them. It's for those who are unable or unwilling to take the risk of starting their own business. It's for those anxious about redundancy at work. It's about choosing to adopt a radically different approach to spending, saving and investing to almost everyone in the UK (and across the wider world). We've labelled those of us who fit this description, and who choose to change their lives by chasing down the Everest goal of financial independence, as *non-trepreneurs*.

Our life circumstances are likely to differ from your own, perhaps drastically. We have no children, for example. We both worked in corporate jobs for several years and we live in a small town in the English midlands. That doesn't mean those with children, working non-corporate jobs or living in London can't pull off the same trick of early financial independence. We've given examples throughout the book of people who have managed to achieve independence under far more difficult circumstances than our own. We've also pointed you in the direction of other books, blogs, podcasts and video blogs. We've found these all useful in building our knowledge, motivation and self-confidence over the years.

To avoid confusion, this book's been written in my voice (Jason), but it's been a collaboration between both Julie and me. While I wrote the original manuscript, Julie has edited it, several times for her sins! We are, of course, both individuals and have different opinions about personal finance but overall, the content reflects both of our points of view.

Thanks for buying our book, we hope it proves useful, and we wish you the best of luck on your own financial freedom journey.

Jason and Julie

Part One: The Non-Trepreneurs

*"If you will live like no one else,
later you can live like no one else."*

Dave Ramsey, American Personal Finance Broadcaster

Our lives felt normal, we had no reason to be unhappy. We had good jobs, which we'd been lucky to keep while a financial crisis raged across the world. Although we'd chosen not to have children, but we'd followed the script otherwise. We were both in our late 30s, had a three-bedroom detached house, a campervan, Julie had a company car and I had one we owned, we had a garage full of bikes, tools and gym equipment. A hot tub bubbled away in the garden. We were successful but, invisibly to others, I was suffering increasing anxiety and could feel myself sinking into depression.

Something had to change. We eventually opted to quit work, sell, give away or store our belongings, rent our house out and use savings to travel Europe and North Africa in an old motorhome. For two years we roamed, completely free. In that time, we came across people we'd never have met in our normal lives. Many of them were retired through the traditional route, using one or more pensions, but a few weren't. They were relatively young but had freed themselves of the need to work, for ever. Wow! We were completely fascinated, blown away. How? How on Earth had they done it?

Some had built up and sold businesses, a route which I'd considered all my life but had never had the idea, confidence or courage to try it. Others had managed it without owning a business though, and we were intrigued. Through a few snippets of information, we started to learn that they achieved this huge goal by living their lives differently to the norm. They were outwardly indistinguishable from those around them, but the way they saw the world, saw themselves and their finances were all radically different. Meeting a few of these couples drove our interest in a new direction. We'd been considering shifting into low-stress, low-paid jobs to take our lives forwards once our savings were consumed by travel. These individuals offered another path, one which we'd follow to eventually find ourselves in the same position as them, free of the mandatory need to work, for ever.

What is a Non-Trepreneur?

The key thing which attracted us to these individual's stories was this: their approach looked like it could work for us. They'd used their jobs to free them from their jobs.

These *non-trepreneurs* had used their existing earning capability to power their freedom, without the need to become an entrepreneur. None of them had thought up or implemented a new, winning product or service. Instead, they'd used the skills they already had, refined and enhanced perhaps, but fundamentally they already held the key to personal freedom: their day job.

Non-trepreneurs buy their freedom like this: they work to create excess income from their weekly or monthly pay and invest it cash-generating assets. These assets eventually pay all their bills and then some, for life. This income without working is sometimes referred to as *passive income*, as you first actively do the work, but then get paid for it over and over, when you're not doing much, if any, work on it.

If you know where to look, there are examples of non-trepreneurs removing their 9-to-5 (increasingly 8-to-6) restraints early in their lives, often in the 30s or 40s. They go on to either semi-retire (working part-time or working for a few months at a time), fully retire, or change careers to jobs they prefer to do. Some carry on

Part One: The Non-Trepreneurs

working the day job they love with the life-affirming knowledge that they and their loved ones are safe should the day job decide it no longer wants them, or they no longer want it.

My wife Julie and I discovered more about these non-trepreneurs when we came across *the FIRE movement*. FIRE, sometimes written as F.I.R.E or FI/RE, stands for Financial Independence Retire Early, a label which was originally applied to bloggers in the United States but has since spilled out across the world. Some FIRE advocates use business income to power their financial freedom, but many aren't entrepreneurs, earning, saving and investing on a slow-burn, decades-long path to building a life-long nest egg.

We'd already unwittingly adopted some aspects of this way of life for our entire adult lives. Coming from frugal households, neither of us were big spenders. We were brought up with an inherent fear of credit. However, only in our early 40s were we exposed to the critical idea that we could deliberately design our lives to enable us to live without our corporate jobs, and we set about that goal in earnest. Having done much of the leg work in our previous two decades of work, our escape from the corporate cubicle took only a further two whirlwind years.

Julie and I are just one example of a couple using this approach, and our personal experience will be of limited use to some people. Our set of life circumstances, such as the fact we have no children, will be far removed from those of some readers. For this reason, we'll also draw on the writings of other non-trepreneurs out there, referencing the best stories, blogs and books we've come across.

From years of reading these resources, we've come to understand that non-trepreneurs come from a range of backgrounds, some middle class, some from abject poverty. Many have no children, but many have families or choose to start them once they're financially-free. Some are engineers, accountants, managers or doctors, while others are firemen, teachers or work in the military. They're located around the world. Some have degrees, some don't. They don't have much in common but for their non-trepreneur approach to finance and life.

We, along with our fellow non-trepreneurs, occasionally pop-up in the mainstream media, typically with stories about couples who've given it all up to travel the world. These articles tend to be short and punchy, they only scratch the surface, understandably designed more to pull in readers than to explain the underlying drivers and mechanics going on under the surface. To really grasp what these people do differently, and why, this book will dig much deeper.

How Do They Do It?
Looking back at one of those articles, there's often a photo of a couple stood smiling with a beautiful backdrop, like us on the front cover of this book, enjoying the dunes of Erg Chebbi in Morocco. Look a little closer at the cover, nothing out-of-the-ordinary seems to reveal itself? We just look like a happy couple on holiday. We don't appear unusual in any way. We don't look rich. We don't appear to have designer clothes or Breitling watches? Questions may pop into your head: did we inherit a fortune? Win the lottery? Write a chart-topping song? Create and sell a business? Of course, we didn't do any of these.

The journalists writing articles on financial independence will tell you how the smiling couple pulled off what's made to seem like either a magic trick, pure luck, or an act of monk-like abstinence. The truth is they tend to earn higher than average salaries, have somehow avoided spending all their income and instead saved a high percentage of it, steadily investing until their assets generated enough money to cover all their life expenses. At this point work became optional for those smiling couples, as it did for Julie and me.

At this level of detail, getting financially-free is as simple and straightforward as going from overweight to a healthy weight. Eat less, exercise more, and boom! Sooner or later your waistline will shrink, those old jeans will fit again, your heart will breathe a sigh of relief and you'll feel magnificent. We all know it's not that simple though.

The devil lives in the detail, and in the fact each of us are predisposed to attack these problems in different ways. No change is possible or permanent without a shift in mindset, indelibly altering how we see ourselves, who we think we are, followed by deliberate, long-term, sustained action. This isn't easy for anyone, but the good news for us was this: once we understood what we needed to do and accepted the challenge, success proved all-but-inevitable. We set about informing ourselves in a determined and relentless way, requiring significant effort to start but later becoming such second nature we hardly realised we were living an unusual, financially fit life.

To my mind, anyone seeking financial freedom needs to know the level of effort required to get the challenge in perspective, and to accept it. Using the fitness analogy again, to burn off 1Kg of body fat requires running roughly 100 miles (or eating 7000 fewer calories, or still better mixing up the two approaches). That's not an easy ask, but if we imagine we can lose that 1Kg by taking a 10-minute stroll each day, we'll soon lose motivation as the results fail to materialise. Unless we see the size of the challenge for what it is, we'll never achieve it.

On the money side of things, we all start out naked in life, tiny and fragile creatures, with not a bean to our names. If we're very lucky, our parents might start investing for us as infants, creating a windfall which covers university tuition fees, rent and beer money. Should you find yourself in this fortunate circumstance of not being loaded down with student loans in your early 20s, you're still looking at over 50 years of 9-to-5 work even if you manage to save 10% of your income for those five decades.

This is a critical point: that 10% figure is largely accepted in British society, it's the norm, even a quite a high amount 'to give up' from your pay. Say you're able to ignore that advice (and have enough income to do so) and aggressively crank up your savings rate to 50% of your take-home income, then your working life drops to under 20 years.

This is going to be hard, almost impossible if you're on a lower income, where necessities eat up most if not all your money. For many of us though, it's rendered hard not by lack of money but by lack of ability to save, or lack of knowledge on how to successfully invest. For those few of us aware, practiced and motivated enough, a 50% savings rate (or even higher) proves entirely possible. An element of luck doesn't do any harm either, but don't rely on it.

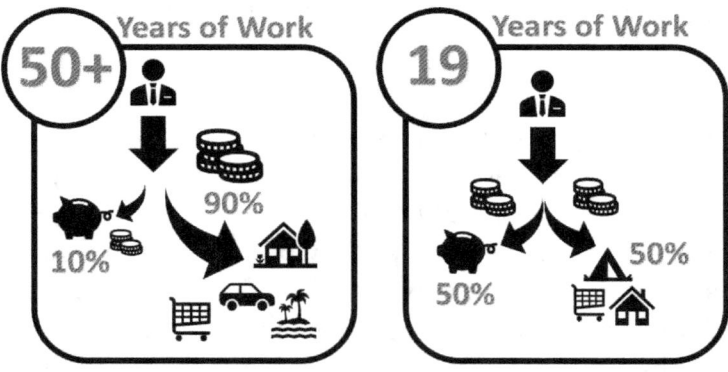

Typically, we might spend 90% of our income and save 10%, which requires 50 years of work. If we can change the balance to 50-50, retirement comes down to as low as 19 years.

One common objection to the FIRE movement, from journalists in particular, is this need to save a high percentage of your income. Some cite the average disposable household income in the UK

Part One: The Non-Trepreneurs

(£31,400)[1] and point out how today's high cost of living eats every penny. I get it. The journalists are writing for a broad audience, but neither going from overweight to marathon fit nor saving a high percentage of our income are *average* activities. They're both *outlier* activities, far outside the norm. No-one is expecting everyone in the UK to suddenly start saving 50% of their income and retiring at 40.

In the UK, around two thirds of adults are overweight or obese[2]. 12.5 million UK households (of the 28 million in total) have either nothing or less than £1,500 in savings. Each house owes on average £4,264 in unsecured debt[3] (typically non-mortgage loans and credit cards). This is an important lesson for us all. No-one becomes a successful non-trepreneur by following the lead of those around us: we must swim against a very strong tide.

At this point we need to tackle one sticky point: debt, and more precisely consumer debt, credit cards, store cards and unsecured loans for example. I've not covered anything specifically about clearing debt. Consumer debt is the enemy, like trying to swim against the tide weighed down with lead bricks. The methods we'll describe about tracking your spending and improving your salary will help generate the excess income needed to fend off the debt devil. But the specific psychology and techniques of debt management aren't covered in this book. Just be aware that it makes no sense to start investing until you've cleared high interest loans, store and credit cards.

---

[1] *www.ons.gov.uk/peoplepopulationandcommunity/personalandhousehold finances/incomeandwealth/bulletins/householddisposableincomeandinequality/fi nancialyearending2021*
[2] *commonslibrary.parliament.uk/research-briefings/sn03336*
[3] *themoneycharity.org.uk/money-statistics*

Why Become a Non-Trepreneur?

There are two questions here: Question 1: why chase off down this less-trodden path of financial freedom? Question 2: why not do it by becoming an entrepreneur? Let's briefly look at them both.

Answer 1: Why the less-trodden path? To regain control over the single most valuable, irreplaceable resource in our lives: our time. In her book *The Top Five Regrets of the Dying*, palliative care nurse Bronnie Ware tells us one of the main regrets people close to death have is: "I wish I hadn't worked so hard"[4].

It came as a naïve shock to me some years ago to realise some people go through their entire lives anxious, stressed-out, unfulfilled and unhappy, and then they die. What a terrible loss, an enormous waste of potential. I started to strive to avoid this disaster befalling me too, searching for ways in which I could live an extra-ordinary life, one in which I could chase down my dreams.

For some, another significant motivation is the desire to have a smaller footprint on the planet. By lowering their consumption, they get the triple benefits of:

- saving more money,
- being surrounded by less clutter,
- and impacting the wider environment less.

For Julie and I, this is simply a win-win scenario. As a natural result of the way we live, we drive far fewer miles, live in smaller spaces, consume less power, replace our clothes and gadgets less often and fly infrequently. Of course, we're not perfect, it just happens that living a simpler, lower-impact life gifts us the increased freedom we crave.

---

[4] *www.theguardian.com/lifeandstyle/2012/feb/01/top-five-regrets-of-the-dying*

Part One: The Non-Trepreneurs

Answer 2: Why not become an entrepreneur? Well, ideally, I would have done just that! I'd have loved to have come up with, created and marketed a brilliant product, providing both employment to others and a service to the community. I simply didn't have either the creativity or the courage. The idea of being an entrepreneur lodged in a corner of my mind almost from the start of my career, getting stronger as the years passed, drawing my attention away from the non-trepreneur approach and in doing so delaying the point I regained life control by years.

I have friends and family who are entrepreneurs. They are inventive, energetic and resourceful, masters of their destiny, and they provide employment and inspiration for their employees. I look up to them, but I couldn't see how I could replicate their achievements, and in the end, I simply didn't need to.

Through these close acquaintances I also discovered the terrific toll being a business owner can take, the stomach-churning anxiety they endured, the risks of losing their family homes and livelihoods. Many new businesses fail, as some of theirs had over time (over half of new businesses don't survive to five years old[5]). Being an entrepreneur can be a wonderful thing for humanity, I believe, but we shouldn't deceive ourselves that it doesn't come at a price.

Who Can Become a Non-Trepreneur?

This is a hard question to answer, one I've wrestled with over the years. In one sense, anyone can, especially if you define someone as being a non-trepreneur as soon as they start on the path to financial independence. There's huge benefit to be found in each stage, regardless of whether you get to the magical *full freedom* end stage. Someone who manages to amass three months of expenses in an emergency fund will place themselves in an incredibly strong

---

[5] *www.ons.gov.uk/businessindustryandtrade/business/ activitysizeandlocation/bulletins/businessdemography/2018*

position compared to most. Their stress levels will reduce, they'll feel more comfortable to take some risk, allowing new opportunities to appear from nowhere, and they'll place themselves further and further beyond the grasp of the debt-peddlers.

But let's not kid ourselves. The gleaming diamond which catches most attention is the end game: gaining the simply incredible, life-affirming position as a financially-free individual. Reaching that point is tough though, very tough. Even for those earning above average incomes it's hard to achieve as the temptation to spend everything is so strong. For those on lower incomes, the need to cover necessities alone will eat up large parts of their money, drastically reducing the capacity to save.

To get examples of who can become a non-trepreneur we can look at people who are either on the path or have completed it and are living on 'the other side', by taking to Google and searching for *FIRE Blogs*. FIRE stands for Financial Independence Retire Early, and it's become attached to anyone seeking financial independence either through the entrepreneur or non-trepreneur approaches. You'll find hundreds of websites, with some of the most established and respected based in North America:

- *earlyretirementextreme.com* – often referred to as ERE, this blog was founded in 2007 and is the original FIRE blog, written by Jacob Lund Fisker. Jacob, a theoretical physicist, advocates a highly frugal, low-consumption lifestyle, one in which we learn and practice life skills rather than outsourcing.
- *www.mrmoneymustache.com* – perhaps the most famous FIRE blogger in the world, software engineer Pete Adeney retired aged 30 and started his hard-hitting website in 2011, in which he advocates frugality, commuting by bicycle and investing in stock market index funds.
- *financialsamurai.com* – Sam Dogen quit his financial job at 34 with a relatively high net worth to cover his family's high cost

Part One: The Non-Trepreneurs

of living in San Francisco. His blog focusses on increased income and investing, rather than on frugality.
- *millennial-revolution.com* – Kristy Shen grew up in rural China, living on a family budget of $0.44 a day. They were able to emigrate to Canada where Kristy became an engineer and they built up an investment nest egg of $1m Canadian Dollars in nine years (around £580,000), before quitting work to travel.

UK offerings include:

- *theescapeartist.me* – Ex-accountant Barney Whiter 'escaped the prison camp' aged 43, with three children. His blog discusses the maths of early retirement, investing strategy and the mindset behind financial freedom, all from a UK-perspective.
- *thehumblepenny.com* - Ken Okoroafor, father of two, describes himself as a Millennial, Migrant, Minority. His story is one of graft and self-belief. With the odds stacked against him, he and his family achieved financial freedom at 34.
- *monevator.com* – written by two anonymous UK bloggers, this site offers up useful and well-crafted posts about earning, spending and investing, backed up with a series of motivational messages.

The people behind these blogs have a strong tendency towards being middle class professionals. Some have kids, some don't, some wait until they're financially independent to have them. They mostly earn above-average incomes. They tend to be engineers, doctors, managers or work in finance, although they also include firemen, teachers and members of the armed forces.

This doesn't mean they all started out in these positions. Some come from a background of poverty, which they turned into a driving force in their lives: they grafted as they clawed their way upwards. In my case, I'm stood on the shoulders of giants. In reality, it took two generations for me to become financially free at 43. My father suffered in childhood and could have adopted the same self-centred, destructive and abusive mindset of his parents, but didn't, luckily for me. Through the hardest of work at farms, coal mines and factories, he proved himself better. My mother's mum died when she was 12 and her father abandoned her and her five siblings, effectively orphaning them. She too worked hard, first as a mother with two small children, isolated, with practically no money and zero support, later in a clothes factory and finally as a home help for the elderly. Between the two of them they quietly transformed their lives and the lives of their children, something I'll be forever grateful for.

None of this means these are the only types of people who can become a successful non-trepreneur of course, just that these are the people writing publicly about it. Personal finances are a taboo subject for most of us (who knows the details of their parents', siblings' or friends' finances?), and a good many of the blogs are written anonymously, making it difficult to work out personal details about the authors' stories.

Another approach to see who can become a non-trepreneur is to look for studies into 'normal' people who've managed to amass wealth. Perhaps the most famous example is the book *The Millionaire Next Door* by researchers Thomas J. Stanley and William D. Danko. The book is subtitled *The Surprising Secrets of America's Wealthy*, with the main secret being that these millionaires are unexpectedly frugal. Some are non-trepreneurs, building their wealth from their jobs either as employees or more likely self-employed professionals, while others are true entrepreneurs. They all tend to live their lives focussing on what's critical to them, ignoring the siren song of status consumerism, avoiding debt, spending relatively little on clothing, watches and cars, saving more than they earn and investing it in appreciating assets. In other words, they act very differently to most Americans, and they don't look how most Americans think rich people should look.

Part One: The Non-Trepreneurs

The authors made a clear distinction between wealth and income. They pointed out that it's very possible to have a high income but not be wealthy. If someone earns £1m a year but spends £1.2m, their wealth will decrease, eventually to the point of bankruptcy. High income doesn't necessarily translate into high wealth, and the authors were surprised to find that many American millionaires lived in blue collar (working class), rather than white collar (middle class) neighbourhoods. They reasoned that the social pressure to demonstrate their wealth was so much lower in these areas, enabling them to live comfortably alongside their neighbours while quietly saving and investing significant sums of money.

The Millionaire Next Door was published in 1996 and updated in 2016 with *The Next Millionaire Next Door* (which was completed by Sarah Stanley Fallaw, Dr. Thomas J. Stanley's daughter after he was killed by a drunk driver). Both books discuss the results of surveys of American millionaires and came to similar conclusions. These studies were separated by 20 years, but the underlying traits involved remained the same: hard work, perseverance, planning and self-discipline. Stock markets, politics and interest rates all changed during those two decades, but the same behaviours produced the same results.

These traits ring true to me, they're timeless. When I picked up a copy of the 96-year-old book *The Richest Man in Babylon* by George S. Clayson, the same age-old lessons were held within those pages, although expressed in a very different way. George uses a collection of parables to discuss topics around only investing in what you understand, saving for the long-term and living within your means.

My feeling is the question you will certainly be asking yourself is whether you personally can achieve the big goal, the final stage of complete freedom. My answer to this is that only you can know, no-one else. Journalists, finance experts, your parents and friends, might all have your best interests at heart (or their own: you decide), but unless they've done it themselves, very few of them are likely to come out and say: "yeah, you can do it, go for it!". In truth, you must make a whole series of uncommon things happen to get free, and none of them are going to occur unless you get started. The self-belief you'll need to see it through builds as you progress, at least that's how it worked out for us.

How Can We Earn Our Freedom?

Let's take another look at the definition of a non-trepreneur, extending it a little: someone who's able to use their job income to buy cash-generating assets which eventually cover all their costs, freeing them from the need to work for money.

The inspiration for Julie and I, and for many of you I suspect, was to gain full financial freedom, to buy our complete self-determination. No-one tells us where we need to be each day. We have no managers to report to. We have no clients to pander to. Put simply, we can do what the hell we please.

Do you need to go all out like we did though? Of course not, you're free to deploy the approach to whatever extent suits you. There are advantages right from the start of the process, even if you opt to retire in your late 60s, life stress is reduced as soon as you start to gain financial self-control.

There is no single path to follow. We'll each come at it in our own way, but the following series of stages might represent an idealised approach, which I would adopt if starting again from scratch. In the real world, these stages will become inter-mingled and some stages might be revisited several times.

Part One: The Non-Trepreneurs

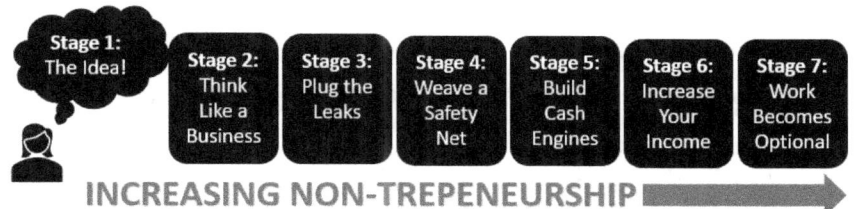

Let's look at each stage in turn.

STAGE 1: The Idea! The first stage is the realisation that achieving financial independence is even possible. We don't HAVE to spend practically everything we earn. We CAN learn to invest. It's POSSIBLE to retire from our careers many years or even decades early. Being HAPPY is entirely possible without owning the big house, the cars and latest array of gadgets.

STAGE 2: Think Like a Business. The next stage is to accept that the sort of results we're talking about don't just happen. They require us to start treating our household finances a little like we're running a small business. We might not be entrepreneurs, but in terms of our income and spending, we need to think like small business accountants, tracking our spending carefully and keeping a close eye on everything we owe and own.

STAGE 3: Plug the Leaks. This stage gets us focussed on the information generated by Stage 2. Where is all our income going? What options do we have to avoid so much of our money running through our fingers like sand? We take a step backwards at this point and really examine our spending from a high level. Do we really, truly need the size of house we have? What about owning two cars? A garage full of stuff? Eating out twice a week? An Amazon-powered shopping habit? Are these 100% necessary, or would we prefer the life-affirming status and power of being financially independent?

The Non-Trepreneurs

STAGE 4: Weave a Safety Net. Now we use the excess cash freed up from Stage 3 to weave a strong safety net below us. This stage gets us into a secure position, insuring against disaster by building a personal emergency fund. Some non-trepreneurs colourfully refer to this 3 to 6-month pot of protection cash (plus the subsequent assets we'll build in Stage 5) as *F*** You Money*. Why? Because it enables the owner of these funds to tell their boss what to do should they become too unreasonable! This is a position of real personal power.

STAGE 5: Build Cash Engines. Now we begin to more strongly deviate from the standard path of 'poor' thinking to the parallel path of 'rich' thinking. Here we gain an understanding that most of us are ploughing our money, our life blood, into depreciating assets. Meals out, TV subscriptions, fashion clothing, cars and luxury holidays. These retain no residual financial value, or rapidly lose it after purchase. Once we grasp this, we can start to build our personal finance knowledge. We can then begin investing for the long-term in appreciating assets like shares, bonds and property, mimicking the approach taken by the quietly wealthy among us.

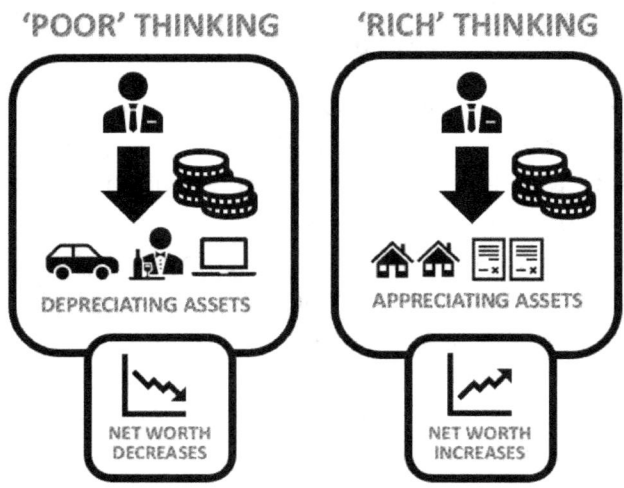

Part One: The Non-Trepreneurs

> *Constant advertising pressures us to buy depreciating assets: cars, clothes, luxury holidays, gadgets, meals out. The quiet rich ignore much of this. They divert their income into appreciating assets like rental property, bonds and shares.*

STAGE 6: Increase Your Income. The more you earn, the more opportunity you have to save, accelerating the rate at which you can invest and reducing your mandatory working life. While you can only cut your life expenses so far, there is no upper limit to how much you can earn. Non-trepreneurs typically increase their income through a range of strategies, depending on their situation. Some simply ask for a raise. Some change companies. Some work overtime. Some take night classes to increase their market value. Some go self-employed. Some use their skills to moonlight, running night-classes for example, or start a side gig that they can do in their spare time.

STAGE 7: Work Becomes Optional. Our lives are now simplified and focussed on what's crucial for our happiness and sense of belonging in the world around us. Our investments generate enough money on an ongoing basis to cover all our life expenses, for as many years as we may live. We no longer HAVE to work for a living, if we CHOOSE not to. We're FREE to try out a career change with massively diminished risk, to stay at home with young children, to travel, to take care of loved ones, to volunteer our time for projects important to us, whatever we find fulfilling and meaningful. Once we reach the end of this stage we've topped out and are stood taking in the views from the mountain top, we're full-on non-trepreneurs, only the question of what we do with the rest of our lives remains. This is a great position to be in!

Our experience has included all these stages, albeit with twists and turns, with an additional (completely optional) stage tagged on to the end: becoming small-scale entrepreneurs. Once the pressure to earn was eased, and the financial penalty of failure was removed, we found that we enjoyed writing about our travel experiences, blogging and self-publishing books, all of which give us purpose and enjoyment, and generate an additional income over and above our core investments.

How Long Does the Path Take?

We'll go into mindset in more detail in Part Two of the book, but one key element is long-term thinking. Start thinking in years, not days, weeks or months. Ideally think in decades. I'm not trying to scare you or put you off, our own shift from employees aged 41 to being financially-free only took two years, although we'd been inadvertently working towards it for two prior decades. When we finally started deliberately tackling the problem, we still expected it to take another five to ten years (revising the time down as we reduced our income goal). We now have (hopefully) many decades to live from this point onwards, so we also need a long-term frame of mind to be sure our financial plan will continue to support us to the grave.

One way for you to answer the question of 'how long' is to look at your savings rate. This is the percentage of your take-home income which you're able to save into either your emergency fund or, once you've filled that, into investments. Let's say you're a couple both working full-time, earning the same amount and you save the entirety of one of your salaries, so you have a 50% savings rate. Starting from a position of no assets, and no debt, it would take under 20 years to amass enough investments to generate all the income you need for the rest of your life[6]. These calculations assume you're investing in equities (shares and bonds), but you can do similar calculations yourself for rental property, for example.

---

[6] *theescapeartist.me/2016/01/21/the-3-numbers-that-can-make-you-a-millionaire*

Part One: The Non-Trepreneurs

Curiously this rule-of-thumb applies regardless of how much you earn. With a 50% savings rate, a typical figure in the FIRE blogger world, it would take the same number of years for a couple on £18,000 each, as it would for a couple earning £100,000 each. Why is this? Because those on higher incomes are spending more than those on lower ones, and therefore still need the same amount of time to build a bigger pot of investments to cover their higher ongoing costs. The following table gives you a range of savings rates along with the number of years you will need to work while saving that percentage before you are able to retire.

Savings Rate	Years to Retirement
15%	56
20%	47
30%	34
40%	25
50%	19
60%	14
70%	10
80%	6
90%	3
100%	0

Different sources use differing assumptions for this table, resulting in slightly different numbers of years, but the overall concept remains the same: a higher savings rate drastically reduces the mandatory number of working years. The calculations in this table make the following assumptions, all of which are important to understand:

- Your incomes won't go up faster than inflation (if they do, and you don't spend more as a result, you could retire sooner).
- You won't have any bonuses or windfalls (again if you do, and don't spend them, you'll retire faster).
- You'll earn 5% annual return on your investments in real terms (your actual returns would have to be higher to allow for

inflation). If you earn only 4%, then a 30% savings rate equates to 39 years of work, not 34.
- You'll spend 4% of the value of your investments the first year you 'retire', with that figure rising with inflation.
- All your money is invested outside of a personal pension, so you're able to access it before age 55. I'm not suggesting you do this, but we'll work this way here just for the purpose of keeping this calculation simple.
- You won't earn any additional income after retirement (if you expect to receive a state pension then you could retire earlier).
- And finally, no-one else will support you in retirement.

How Much Money Do You Need

Just how much money do people who manage to retire early have? There's a clue (very well) hidden in the previous section. In the assumptions we said this couple would live on 4% of their investments in the first year they 'retire', rising with inflation. This percentage comes from research into historical stock and bond returns and is called the Safe Withdrawal Rate (SWR). We'll come back to the SWR later, on page 133.

Let's say from tracking your spending you know you'll need £25,000 a year to live on, and to have a fulfilling life, and are convinced this will be enough in your retirement years. To get that £25,000, you can use this calculation to work out roughly how much you'll need invested:

(100 ÷ SWR) x Yearly Expenses = **Your Investment Target**

So, in this example, with a 4% SWR:

(100 ÷ 4) x 25,000 = **£625,000**

That's the amount you'll need in investments alone, not including the value of any non-cash-generating assets like your home or car. More conservative non-trepreneurs use an SWR of 3%, making the investment target 33.3 x 25,000 which is £833,333, and a few even go as low as 2%, making the target 50 x 25,000 = £1.25m.

As you can see, we're not talking about small numbers! Some FIRE bloggers have investments valued at multi-million pounds (or more usually US dollars). Sam at *financialsamurai.com* and his wife had $3m when he retired from his corporate finance career in 2012[7].

That said, some have extremely low costs of living given the countries they live in. Jacob at *earlyretirementextreme.com* lives in the US and spends roughly $7,000 a year (£5,700)[8]. His wife spends the same amount but continued to work to cover her expenses. At an SWR of 4%, Jacob would need 25 x 7,000 which equals $175,000 (£142,500) to retire, and it took him only five years to get there on a researcher's salary[9]. Pete at *mrmoneymustache.com* and his wife retired from their software engineering jobs with total assets of around $900,000 (£690,000), and it took them ten years to get there[10].

Where Does this Wealth Come From?
The wealth mostly comes from two places:

1. Money saved from job income.
2. Income from investments.

As discussed earlier, the higher your savings rate, the quicker you'll amass the money you need, but while most non-trepreneurs are relatively high earners, more income doesn't necessarily shorten your working life. In my job I worked alongside people who made a similar income to me, but who had a house much, much bigger

---

[7] *www.financialsamurai.com/financial-samurai-net-worth-and-retirement-income*
[8] *earlyretirementextreme.com/how-i-live-on-7000-per-year.html*
[9] *He's since sold over 40,000 copies of his Early Retirement Extreme book.*
[10] *www.mrmoneymustache.com/2011/09/15/a-brief-history-of-the-stash-how-we-saved-from-zero-to-retirement-in-ten-years*

than they needed (in my humble opinion), at least one luxury car each, a horse and horse box, designer clothes, frequent expensive meals out and high-end holidays. I've no idea how much they managed to save, but I can't imagine they had a high savings rate.

Non-trepreneurs use a simple but effective tactic called 'paying yourself first' to help them save. When their salary arrives, they deduct savings *before* they pay their bills. They then use whatever is left for discretionary spending. In this way they never 'see' the savings as money available to be spent. Julie and I used this psychological trick when saving into our pensions in our 20s and 30s, as the payroll department deducted the contributions before paying us, and we never 'missed' the money.

With the money saved from your job income, once you've any non-mortgage debt paid off and have an emergency fund in place, you can (and should) start to invest, and the right investments will quickly start to generate additional income, which again you can (and should) re-invest.

I'm not talking about saving cash into a current account, which will generate little in interest these days. I'm talking about investing in shares, bonds, rental property or a combination of these. For example, if you owned shares in a fund 'tracking' the FTSE 100 (the 100 largest companies in the UK) between 1984 and 2019 you'd have seen an annual average return of 7.8%[11] (a combination of the increase in share price plus dividend payments to shareholders). The Standard & Poor 500 (the 500 largest US companies) returned an annual average of 10.6% between 1957 and 2021[12]. We'll come onto index tracking (passively managed) funds on page 126.

---

[11] *www.ig.com/uk/trading-strategies/what-are-the-average-returns-of-the-ftse-100--200529*

[12] *www.investopedia.com/ask/answers/042415/what-average-annual-return-sp-500.asp*

Part One: The Non-Trepreneurs

As of early 2019, one platform investing in UK property calculated an average return (rent plus capital increase) of 6.66% over the previous decade[13]. For the examples in this book, we'll use an average long-term annual investment return of 7%. This is just an example figure: each of us will receive different long-term returns which will also vary year on year, including some years where your portfolio crashes, and some where it booms.

Over several years, these percentages will also *compound up*, meaning you're earning *interest on interest*. Over non-trepreneurial timescales (decades), this compounding makes an eye-popping difference to your wealth. Let's have a look at an example. In the graph below, two different households both consistently save £25,000 a year for 30 years, so put the exact same amount of money into their investments.

The first household saves cash in 0% accounts. This cash is not compounded (as there is no interest), and the line ends at £750,000 after 30 years. However, the second invests in a fund inside a stocks and shares ISA, earning an average of 7% a year, which is then reinvested. After around 10 years this investment starts to quickly outstrip the cash equivalent, at a faster and faster rate, taking off like a fighter jet. After 30 years the compounded wealth has powered its way to a total of £2.3m, an enormous difference.

---

[13] *www.propertypartner.co/blog/uk-residential-property-market-index-february-2019*

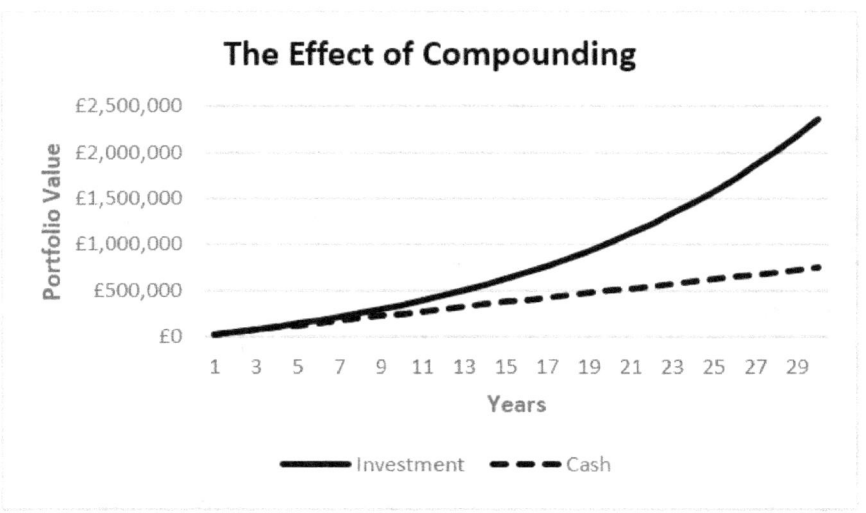

To get the gains of compounding you should ideally start investing as early as possible in your working life. As you can see in the graph above, both lines follow a similar path for the first decade. Only after that does the compounding line really start to accelerate upwards. The compound effect takes time to work.

Another way to look at this is to take two investors, both now aged 55. Both invested £5,000 a year for five years during their earlier lives, and then contributed nothing more, making no withdrawals, allowing the investment to compound up at 7%. They both invested the same amount: £25,000, the only difference is the first investor put their money into the market when they were 25, and the other started investing a decade later, aged 35. What's the result?

Part One: The Non-Trepreneurs

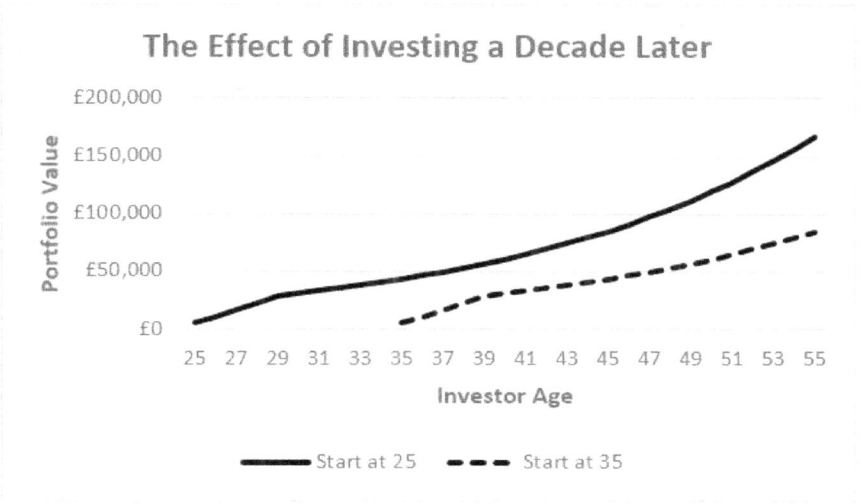

The investor who started at 35 will have grown a pot of £84,000 from their initial £25,000 investment. However, the investor who started at 25 will be sitting on almost double that, over £166,000, having invested the same amount and received the same annual return.

Of course, none of this is easy. The demands on our income are at their highest in our 20s and 30s, as we buy our first cars, take on mortgages, get married and start families. At the same time our earnings won't peak until we're in our 40s[14]. Being able to free up the money to invest for a goal far over the horizon is hard, but if you can do it, you'll reap the rewards later in life.

What's Wrong with Work?

With all this talk about early retirement and being able to stop working, you might imagine I hate work! Some of you reading this will love your job. You'll be fulfilled by it. It will give you a deep sense of purpose, a feeling of security and success, companionship,

---

[14] *www.ons.gov.uk/employmentandlabourmarket/peopleinwork/ earningsandworkinghours/bulletins/annualsurveyofhoursandearnings/2019*

progression and contribution. Others won't have the same sensations, perhaps because they don't like their boss or co-workers, are bored rigid, don't feel valued, can't stand office politics or resent their commute. Research by *Investors in People* showed that in 2019, around a third of UK employees reported being unhappy at work[15]. It's a mixed bag.

In the two decades of 'normal' work I did, it was probably the jobs I did right at the start when I felt most fulfilled. The first was as a labourer on building sites right after I graduated from university, saving up enough money for a round-the-world trip. When I returned, I started a PhD before dropping out and finding a job as a technical author back in the UK, writing about IT systems, which again I enjoyed. I ended up staying in IT, moving jobs every few years and gradually shifting into team leadership and then project management. The jobs were challenging and paid well but attracted an increasing degree of paperwork and international travel, and I started to feel I was missing out on something outside the office.

Julie's story was different to mine, in that she didn't go to university and instead started her career as a secretary. Over the years she gradually accepted opportunities to take on more responsibility, achieved chartered marketeer status after three years of night classes and moved companies a few times too.

Julie enjoyed her work, but she was eventually coerced into a team leader job which she just didn't want. Spending her days in back-to-back meetings rather than doing anything she felt was productive, it eventually wore her down too.

In summary neither of us saw anything wrong with work as such but, since we've made it optional, we've removed many of the

---

[15] *www.investorsinpeople.com/wp-content/uploads/2019/06/Job-Exodus-2019-InvestorsInPeople.pdf*

negative aspects of work, choosing only to do what we enjoy, and have seen our anxiety levels falls massively as a result.

Our Personal Non-Trepreneur Story

Before we adopted the non-trepreneur approach to life, we found ourselves growing despondent with our jobs as we approached our late 30s. We didn't have any children, having decided over the years that we didn't want to start a family. While the idea that we could make a major change in our lives felt frightening, a TV programme called *Pay Your Mortgage off in Two Years* got us started on the path, exciting us into thinking about what could be possible without our mortgage debt hanging over us. The idea of paying the whole amount off was too daunting, so we set a goal of clearing £20,000 from it over the following year.

We started to change our behaviour to enable the savings we needed to make. OK, it was mainly me who needed to change. I'd developed habits over the years of spending on expensive computers, tablet PCs, IT books, tools, motorbikes, tropical fish, a hot tub, you name it. I largely bought them as a reward for working hard but started to see these purchases for what they were: temporary relief from the anxiety and stress of the job.

Around the same time the 2008 financial crisis occurred and pushed interest rates down on our tracker mortgage. The bank offered us a lower monthly repayment, but Julie instead increased it. I called a halt to my spending and we started to clear out some of our unused possessions (the garage and loft were stuffed with them). We were dismayed at just how little it was worth, further reinforcing the determination not to buy any unnecessary new stuff.

Any additional money we got from pay rises or bonuses at work went into the mortgage. In the first year we managed to pay off £26,000, which gave us the motivation to try to completely clear the debt. After two more years the final statement arrived. Balance to pay: £0.00. We'd done it, aged 38, the relief flowed over us, and we started to get excited that the future might hold something other than the office.

We were still taking holidays and spending enough to keep us happy, and all the "mortgage money" now went into our savings account. Despite the great position we were in, pressure seemed to increase at work, and I found myself starting to sink into the dark hole of depression as the months passed, becoming increasingly desperate for a change. The story of the trapped monkey resonates, caught after pushing his hand through a small hole to get a handful of nuts, unable to pull his hand back without letting go of the nuts. I needed to let go, but I was afraid, and trapped.

One evening we sat in the garden and had *the talk*. I'd finally snapped. Tears flowed and we made the (for us) momentous decision to quit work. We'd rent our house out, buy an old motorhome and, hoping it didn't fall apart, drive to Dover, take a ferry to Calais and turn right, planning the route as we went. The following day I resigned, an act I'd fantasised about, but it was quite a sad moment in truth, leaving my teammates and the company I'd worked at for many years. I felt myself stepping into a void, fearful I'd made the wrong choice. Julie resigned a few months later, with the same sensations.

For what turned out to be two years we travelled with our pet dog Charlie across Europe and North Africa in a 20-year-old motorhome we called Dave. The original idea was of a one-year career break, where we'd work out what to do with the rest of our lives while we were away, then come back and resume work in one form or another.

We'd budgeted the trip based on shorter campervan holidays we'd taken while working, and soon discovered long-term travel could be done much more cheaply. Julie started keeping a note of everything we spent, because we knew we'd have to return home

Part One: The Non-Trepreneurs

once our savings were gone. That said, we also realised in the first few weeks that we were being too frugal, and needed to spend more on eating out, tourist attractions, campsites and so on, relatively small things which did a lot to enhance our travelling experience. Although we closely tracked our costs, our weekly budget was increased to force us to spend more, not less. Over those 707 nights we averaged €46 a day for both of us, £21 per person per day.

Although the hot tub, cable TV, Amazon deliveries and in-house gym were all gone, the incredible sensation of freedom more than made up for them. Each evening we'd decide where to go the next day, or to just stay put. There were no deadlines, no meetings, no alarms, no commutes, no demanding bosses, no customers or clients, just us three, doing whatever we pleased. We spent our time discovering. We slept by beaches, castles, villages, cities, lakes, forests, fjords, deserts, ruins, and even on the sides of volcanoes, although we didn't really sleep much on the Vesuvius and Etna nights! We had an absolute blast.

Relaxing by the Adriatic Sea in Croatia

Life in a motorhome isn't the same as in bricks-and-mortar. All the utilities which are plumbed into a house, flowing freely (albeit metered) are restricted in a van, and this taught us to be very careful with all our resources, not just money.

We funded our travels with our savings. We didn't touch income coming in from our rented-out house, as we knew we would need something to tide us over until we found jobs when we got home. We'd also had a small two-bed bungalow rented out, which I'd owned when Julie and I met. We opted to rent it out when we moved out, as the housing market dipped in our area and we struggled to sell it. The rental income covered the repayment mortgage we had on it. Looking back, we had good assets behind us, we just didn't realise it at the time.

When our savings ran out, we came home and started to look for work. The tenants wanted to stay in our house, so we rented a smaller, and cheaper house knowing the rent from our bigger house would cover it. As neither of us had a job when we got back, part of the rental income we'd saved during travelling was needed to pay six months' rent in advance.

While we'd been on the road, we'd met other financially-free folks who later became good friends. One had suggested we read *An Unfair Advantage: The Power of Financial Education* by Robert Kiyosaki, but we'd ignored the recommendation until we were back home. Picking the book up was a revelation and kick-started a reading spree which carries on to this day. While I don't agree with all that Robert says, especially around his aggressive real-estate investing approach, his books did a great job of shaking me up.

Up until this point in life I'd had no interest in personal finance, I found it dull, mystifying even. The desire to be able to resume our travels, to regain our freedom, was strong enough in me to flip a switch and get me engaged in it all. As soon as I read *The Unfair Advantage*, and then *Rich Dad, Poor Dad* (by the same author), I quickly realised I'd a fixed mindset around risk, money and how I fitted into society, which had to change for me to gain my freedom long-term. Robert's approaches to building wealth didn't match ours, but his key point fascinated me: the truly wealthy buy assets, while the middle class buy liabilities. The difference was simple for me to understand, assets would create an income while liabilities cost us money, acting as a ball-and-chain on our personal freedom.

One evening we sat down with a glass of wine, a big blank sheet of paper and some marker pens and set out a plan to build up £25,000 a year in investment income. Over the final weeks of travel, we'd considered and discarded the idea of lower-paid, less stressful jobs. We reasoned we'd relatively high-value skills which were still fresh, a great opportunity to generate the capital we'd need to invest. The idea of going back to the office wasn't palatable to either of us, but that way lay our freedom, and we resolved to give our old careers another (temporary) go.

The plan we drew up would give us relatively secure income streams which would last the rest of our lives. We were only 41 at the time and didn't want to spin the corporate hamster wheel for 20 more years. We performed a 'financial health check' on ourselves, noting down everything we owned. We even pulled our pension paperwork out of the back of a drawer and were surprised to find we'd get around £15,000 a year between us when we reached our pension ages in our 60s. We continued reading, coming across the established FIRE blogs like *Mr Money Mustache, Early Retirement Extreme*, and *JL Collins* which exposed us to the idea of using stock and bond funds to build long-term income. We worked through a range of investment and income-generating strategies, and decided we'd fund them by me working as a freelancer while Julie would look for a full-time job.

Freelancing would mean doing the exact same job I'd done as an employee, an IT project manager, but would mean I'd be effectively working for myself. That meant much less protection: no sick pay, no holiday pay, no job security and no training. I had to insure myself, use an accountant to submit reports to HMRC, and make sure I saved up enough money to pay my taxes at the end of each year. On the plus side, if I could find consistent work, I could effectively double my take-home pay.

Both of us found work within a couple of months of returning home, me as a freelancer back at my old company, and Julie as a permanent employee at a new company. Finding life back in a bricks-and-mortar suburban house uninspiring, we researched the option of living on a narrowboat in a nearby marina. After investigating the pros and cons of such a change, visiting the marina and looking around a few boats, we eventually decided not to follow that route. We were undecided until, for the first time in our lives, we used a spreadsheet to work out the likely impact of a big financial decision. The outcome of a spreadsheet analysis said we'd see our net worth £50,000 lower after a decade on the narrowboat, compared to buying another house (since boats tend to depreciate while houses appreciate). That was enough to shift our focus back towards buying a house. Looking back, we made the right decision, although the narrowboat lifestyle still intrigues us, and we may go down that route in the future.

In between all of this we retrieved all our remaining belongings from storage, which we'd not needed or missed for two years, and set about selling or giving almost all of them away. We'd come to love our old motorhome, which had safely carried us thousands of miles down to the edge of the Sahara, but the time came to sell it too. Gradually we reduced what we owned until we were left only with items we used regularly, retaining just a single *memories box* each of old photos, school reports, certificates and the like.

We re-mortgaged the bungalow we rent out onto an interest-only basis and, combined with work income, we used the capital to buy an old butcher's shop in an adjacent town. We'd no plans to start selling meat for a living, but the shop was part of a three-bedroom

Part One: The Non-Trepreneurs

house with an outbuilding behind it. This meant we could move out of our rental house and we hoped it would offer us an opportunity in one way or another in the future. The property was in the centre of town too, an easy walk to shops, restaurants, pubs, supermarkets, doctors and dentists, a leisure centre, and countryside paths, as well as regular public transport into the city. This was important to us, as it both increased our quality of life and drastically reduced our transport costs. We bought an old but reliable Smart car, which one of us used for commuting, while the other took public transport.

As the money from our jobs flowed in, we kept our outgoings low (mainly by working all hours) and lived off Julie's wage. This enabled us to invest around 80% of our earnings. We started investing in the stock market using stocks and shares ISAs set up through our bank, buying low cost, passive index tracking funds, which spread our money across thousands of companies around the globe (we'll come back to index trackers later in the book). It was both an exciting and terrifying moment when we first hit the button to buy these shares, spending £10,000 just like that. Gulp!

We've since gotten used to buying shares, which we intend to hold for decades, without fear or hesitation. We keep building our knowledge in this area and have lived through a couple of steep market declines (bear markets), one of which saw our portfolio drop roughly £30,000 in just a few days. We didn't panic and sell and are now comfortable with the volatility involved in owning passive index trackers.

We moved into the house behind the ex-butcher's shop and started to renovate the whole building, working maybe 70 hours a week between our day jobs and the refurb. Where we were capable of doing the work ourselves, we did it, including refitting and retiling the bathroom. The rest of the time we used tradesmen to rewire the entire property, move radiators, re-plaster the walls, refit the kitchen and renovate the outbuilding to create a 4th bedroom. It was when we were planning the layout for the extra bedroom that it dawned on us, Instead of living in the house and renting out the outbuilding bedroom with AirBnB or similar, we could move into the outbuilding and rent out the two double bedrooms in the house. This meant we would be living in a much smaller space, but it would increase our rental income and be more practical for when we wanted to be away travelling – we'd simply lock up the outbuilding and go.

During all of this we did practically nothing for fun, and Julie suffered depression as a result. We sat down and had another talk after which we revised down our target passive income target to £20,000 a year, agreeing we'd find paid work if we wanted to do something expensive, like take a cruise to the Antarctic. This enabled Julie to feel comfortable quitting work.

Me refitting the bathroom during the butcher's renovation

After just over a year, we had a small shop we could let out, plus two double bedrooms we could also let, while retaining access to one ensuite room for ourselves to live in when we were in the UK. At this point we were both 43 and had been home for just two years. We'd installed solar panels on the roofs of the butchers and the bungalow, and the combined income from these plus the rent,

Part One: The Non-Trepreneurs

dividend income and other more minor streams tipped us over the £20,000 a year mark.

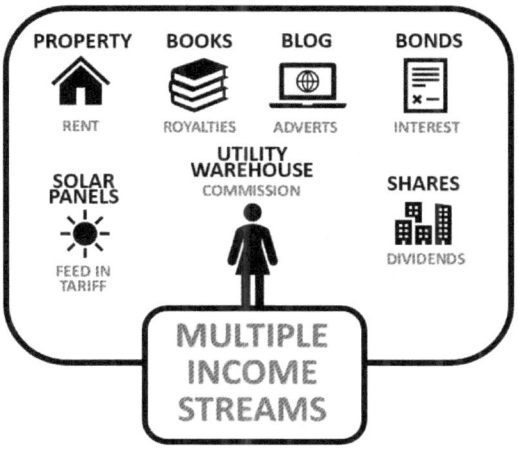

Our income comes from several sources

As we signed the tenancy agreements for the shop and house, the realisation that we'd set ourselves free started to sink in, but it didn't feel real. Had we really set ourselves free of the need to work for ever? We didn't know at the time, and we still don't know for sure, but it looks increasingly likely we're permanently free. It feels surreal that we don't need to work for a living, but our finances are more secure than they were five years ago.

At the point the shop and house rent started to flow, I stopped working and we set off travelling again, buying another motorhome and heading off to Europe and Morocco.

We've now spent over four years on the road. We now travel as and when we want to, with tenants in our home keeping it safe while we're away. Our investments have performed consistently, and in what's turned out to be an interesting twist to the story, we've found ourselves turning a little entrepreneurial too, generating income from advertising on our travel blog and books we've written and self-published.

The Non-Trepreneurs

Us three enjoying spring in Croatia

One of the criticisms of (very) early retirees is that they're not really retired, they all seem to work in one way or another. Some retire for a while then go back to a day job. Some start personal finance blogs which they operate like small businesses, earning from referrals, advertising, consulting services and so on. Some write and sell books. Some self-manage their property portfolios. The implication is that they didn't 'really manage the feat' of generating enough passive income to support themselves for decades. My take on it is this: anyone adopting the non-trepreneurial approach is going to be driven and energetic. We may not start out with a business idea which can fulfil all our financial needs, but once the passive investment income is flowing in, and we've hundreds of hours on our hands, doing some work which we enjoy and can do on our terms seems eminently sensible, fun even!

These days when people ask me what I do, I tell them I'm retired. I used to struggle with this question, since the response is always one of surprise, and as I choose to work writing books, I don't really feel 'retired' in the traditional sense. I could say I'm a landlord, author, blogger or travel writer, but now I find it easier to keep it simple.

In Summary

It's hard, but possible for many of us to stop swapping our time for money much earlier than the normal age in our 60s. Non-trepreneurs do this, removing the need for paid work in their 50s, 40s and even 30s. They achieve it by building up investment income using money from their day jobs:

1. They track and manage expenses like a small business.
2. They have high savings rates, typically 50% or more.
3. They build up an emergency fund.
4. They take the time to financially educate themselves.
5. They increase their income, through self-education, career progression and side-gigs.
6. They then invest to generate long-term passive income.

Eventually the income from their investments is enough to cover their ongoing life expenses, at which point they are financially-free. This gifts them opportunities: to keep working if they want, or to change career, to become a stay-at-home parent, to start a business, to travel, to do whatever they want to, for the rest of their lives.

Part Two: The Freedom Mindset

"Everything is created twice, first in the mind and then in reality."

Robin S. Sharma, Writer and Motivational Speaker

It's only possible to overcome challenges in life once they're framed correctly in your mind. As the saying goes "whether you believe you can or you believe you can't, you're right". Early financial independence requires a good income, a high savings rate and knowledge about long-term, cash-generating investments. But these things all come second. They only occur once the mind is in the right place to enable them to happen. It's important that we see ourselves and the world around us in a way which allows us to accumulate and retain wealth. This part of the book looks at the way a typical non-trepreneur might think, using the inside of my head as an example.

The Standard Mindset

In my native Britain, we're taught to study in our youth, get good qualifications, find a job, buy a house, save 10% of our income, buy the best car, watch and smartphone we can afford, find better jobs, bigger homes and more expensive cars, holiday abroad, upgrade our gadgets, and eventually retire in our 60s. There are some variations around this central theme. Some folks go into self-employment, and some opt to leave education earlier or later than others, but the overall approach remains the same.

Our education system is improving, but still offers little in the way of personal finance education. I was never taught what a credit card was, how a mortgage works, how to think about insurance or inflation or what my pension was invested in. The TV provides a plethora of home buying, building and improvement programs, rarely reflecting on the cost to the buyers in terms of their extended self-enforced working lives. Our government also panders to us all, offering comforting words about how hard life is, and reassuring us they're doing all they can to help. Advertising is everywhere, showing we'll soon be happy, but only if we spend, spend, spend. Offers for credit and store cards are ubiquitous, new cars are now advertised on finance deals at a price per month. Our world tells us that everyone can afford everything, we deserve to have it all.

We're taking this imagined reality at face value. When I was born in 1972, the credit card was a mere six years old in the UK, with the introduction of the Barclaycard in 1966. There are now 59 million of them in use[16] and according to The Money Charity every adult in the country owes an average of £1,369 on their flexible friends, at an average interest rate of over 20%[17]. Excluding student loans, the same charity tells us the average adult in the UK is saddled with £31,845 of debt (including mortgages). Scenes of affluence around us are often funded with borrowed money. Those new cars parked on the neighbourhood driveways? They're probably debt-funded, over 90% of new cars sold by dealers in 2019 were financed[18].

While we're cranking our debt levels up, we're saving less. We've already seen that our savings rate is the key factor determining when we can become financially independent, and that saving 10% of our take-home pay results in a 50-year working life. The actual household savings rate in the UK has been bouncing around the 9% mark for the past decade[19], as shown in the graph below. The result

---

[16] *www.theukcardsassociation.org.uk*
[17] *themoneycharity.org.uk*
[18] *www.fla.org.uk/research/motor-finance-key-statistics*
[19] *obr.uk/box/household-saving-and-debt*

is in an increasing number of retirees reliant on the state pension as their sole means of income.

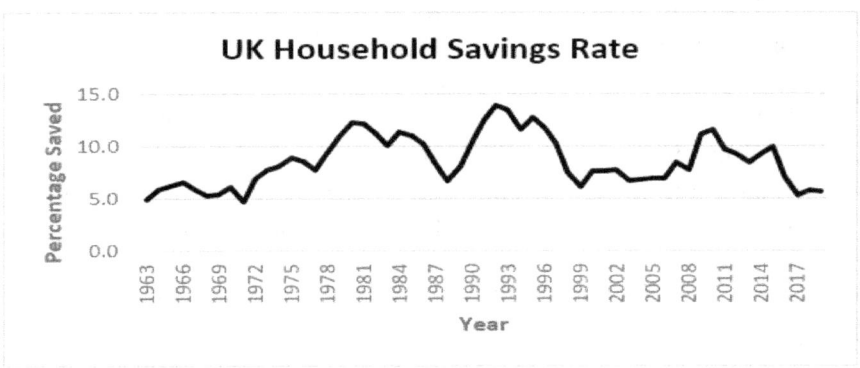

On the other hand, household disposable income (income after income tax, NI and council tax) has been steadily rising in the UK for decades. Even taking inflation into account, the average household income has more than doubled during my lifetime, from £13,368 in 1977 to £29,598 in 2019[20], as shown below.

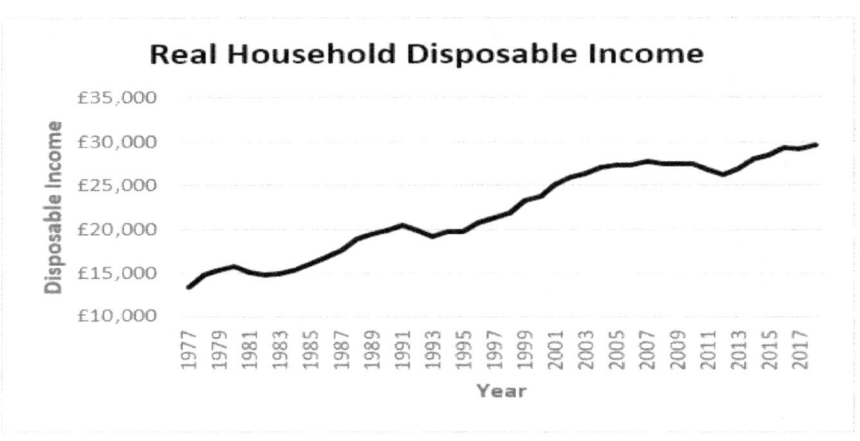

---

[20] www.ons.gov.uk/peoplepopulationandcommunity/
personalandhouseholdfinances/incomeandwealth/bulletins/householddisposablein
comeandinequality/financialyearending2019

There's significant detail hidden behind these averages, of course. There'll be a spread either side, and it's true that the wealthier among us have seen incomes rise much further than the poorer. There are plenty of folks who don't get to share in the rise of wealth across time.

In general though, we're earning more than we ever have, but spending even more than that. Many of the expressions of wealth we see around us: houses, new kitchens, shining cars, wardrobes of designer clothes, the latest smart phones and watches, are funded by debt, they're really owned by the banks. In our collective minds, this is all quietly accepted as the norm.

The Status Mindset

How do you see yourself status-wise? Maybe you see yourself as proud of your working-class background? Perhaps you've attained a good standard of middle-class lifestyle? Wherever you see yourself on the 'social ladder', you probably unconsciously compare yourself with those around you: neighbours, friends, colleagues and family.

There may be a few issues with this. We've already seen how much visible apparent wealth is in truth debt. Unless we discuss the details of our personal finances with friends, family, work colleagues and neighbours, we really have no idea what situation they are in or how well prepared they are for the future.

There's also the fact we're missing a great deal of perspective if we keep our focus so close to the here and now. The late and great Hans Rosling spent his final couple of years (knowing that he was dying) writing the book *Factfulness*, which is well worth a read. In it he points out the great strides being made in worldwide human progress, while at the same time illustrating just how wealthy we are in the UK and Europe. He splits the (very roughly) seven billion population of the planet onto four levels, 1 to 4:

- **Level 1** – one billion people live in extreme poverty, where the dream is to buy a bicycle to make it easier to fetch water and take produce to market.
- **Level 2** – three billion people live here, where the bike dream comes true. They've ditched the wood fire and are cooking on a gas bottle.
- **Level 3** – another two billion live at this level, where they've running water in their homes, perhaps own a motorbike or moped and have two hobs for cooking.
- **Level 4** – this is where the one billion wealthiest people live. We've a car, hot and cold running water in our homes, a varied diet and can afford to take holidays abroad.

If you're living in the UK, you're very likely on level 4, one of the one billion to live at this level. Without the above perspective, most of us will never realise we have a better standard of living than six billion people, regardless of how old our cars are, or whether we can afford that island kitchen refit. Julie and I have spent around six months living and travelling in North Africa, a relatively rich part of the continent, and yet an experience which has made me feel uncomfortably wealthy ever since.

We can also gain perspective by looking backwards. When my parents managed to save up a mortgage deposit, we moved from a rented council house to a terraced house they bought. No-one had a driveway, and I can recall dad buying parts from a scrapyard and fixing his car in the street, a not uncommon sight those days. All the cars parked up one side of the street, allowing emergency vehicles to get by if needed. When I walk past the same house today, both sides of the street are crammed with cars. I never see those cars being fixed in the street, but I do see them in the car wash, being valeted by hand. There were around 19 million cars on UK roads in

1971, and almost double that (around 37 million) today[21], reflecting what's happened on my old street during my lifetime. Yes, the UK population has increased too, but only by around 20%.

I used to worry that I'd feel like a failure in society if I let go of my office job, the suit, the job title, the salary. This status anxiety held me locked into a life which was increasingly crushing me. I'm completely free of that sensation now, I miss none of it, the sense of freedom I have, coupled with the understanding that I'm far better off than my parents and the majority of people in the world, more than makes up for it all.

The Money Mindset

Although I never consciously sat and thought about it, for the first two decades of my adult life I held certain beliefs about money:

- Money doesn't buy happiness.
- Money is for buying stuff or convenience.
- People get wealthy at the expense of others.
- Investing makes no sense, you're risking your money.
- A higher income means I'm more successful.
- Getting into debt is bad.

Although I didn't acknowledge them, these beliefs drove my behaviour around money. Every small spending decision, every opportunity to save, every big lifestyle change was being manipulated by these underlying, unchallenged assumptions.

Were they the right assumptions? Some of them probably were. Debt can be a useful instrument, when used to buy appreciating assets (we'll discuss the concept of leveraging later) but is a path to unhappiness otherwise. The others? Not so much. While money might not lead to happiness, living without enough of it most

---

[21] *www.smmt.co.uk/vehicle-data/motorparc-vehicles-in-use-uk*

certainly leads to unhappiness. Money spent on unused or underused stuff is a wasted opportunity. Once the stuff's bought, most of it quickly renders itself worthless. Money placed in appropriate long-term investments on the other hand slowly multiplies itself.

The fact I associated income with success was a major problem for me. Throughout my career I'd slowly increased my salary, and by the time I became disillusioned I was on a relatively high income, which started to feel more of a trap than a giver of fulfilment. Are income and success really tied together? It depends how you define success, I think. If you define success as the level of self-determination you have, how much you can decide day-to-day how you will spend your time, then a high income could represent a very low level of success. I can recall plenty of stories of my co-workers taking their company smartphones on holiday, sending emails at 3am, even when they should be relaxing, enjoying the time with their families.

The Obstacle Mindset

Life is a series of challenges, problems and obstacles. I recall being in the office, where buzzwords abounded, and being told that we should think of problems as opportunities. I rolled my eyes in irritation, but I was wrong to do so. At the time I perhaps had too many 'opportunities' which I wasn't able to find solutions to. I was stressed stupid.

Later I came across Stoicism while reading the *Mr Money Mustache* blog. Stoicism is a 2000-year-old way of thinking about life, which includes guidance on how to face day-to-day problems. But it was only when I read Ryan Holiday's modern take on the subject in his book *The Obstacle is the Way* that I really grasped what Stoicism was telling me. Ryan used the true-life stories of exceptional people who were arguably made that way by the obstacles they'd faced: Amelia Earhart, Ulysses S. Grant, Steve Jobs and many others.

The message I took from the book was simple: we'll all face a series of challenges in life (some of us will have it easier than others of course) and to be successful we can't shy away from them. Our characters are forged in the fires of difficulty. Getting to financial independence involves overcoming a whole host of obstacles:

- **Saving more of your income.** By ignoring advertising, living well within your means and paying yourself first.
- **Increasing your income.** Some obstacles here: getting qualifications, earning career promotions, negotiating your salary and becoming a leader.
- **Learning to invest.** This requires us to overcome fear, build financial knowledge, understand risk and perhaps become a landlord.

Climbing and summiting a high mountain involves self-belief, preparation, risk, teamwork, practice and sustained effort. If you were dropped on the top by helicopter, the financial equivalent of winning the lottery, will your character have been strengthened by the experience? While many lottery winners hold onto their winnings, some don't. They never faced the obstacles needed to build the mindset and knowledge to manage their newfound wealth and spent or lost it all as a result.

The Control Mindset

Who is in control of your life? Who gets to say what you do and when? Who determines whether you're happy or overly stressed? Who decides your levels of income and debt? Who influences what clothes you wear or car you drive? The answer to all these questions should be you. Not an employer, the government, advertisers or your friends and neighbours. You should be in control of you. That's the real aim of the non-trepreneur, financial independence buys personal control.

The Non-Trepreneurs

Few workplaces are democracies. We don't get to vote for our boss, or their boss. If we join a company under one great manager who we admire, they might be replaced at any time with someone we've never met. These unelected individuals wield enormous power over us. They decide where we can physically be and when for half of our waking lives, how we can be dressed and even what we can and cannot say while we're working for them. They purposefully restrict our ability to spend time off work, typically not letting us spend longer than two weeks away at any one time, which often needs to be booked weeks, if not months, in advance.

The obvious answer to all of this is that we leave, we can walk away, we are free men and women after all. But just how free are we? If the only choice is to move to another similar company, we're most likely stepping from one set of 'control' circumstances to the exact same set elsewhere. We can go self-employed, which brings a degree of increased personal freedom, but at the cost of the comfort blanket provided by full-time employment contracts. Or we can aim for the stars and become non-trepreneurs: cranking up our savings rate, building investments and rendering us gradually more and more free from outside control.

Once we enter adult life, we quickly build up our indebtedness, leaving us with no choice but to work, to keep swapping our time for money. It never even occurs to us what we might do if we no longer had to work for money. I once asked a colleague what they'd do if they no longer had to come into the office, but their wages were still paid. He was struck dumb, sat staring at me. I felt so bad about the episode, I now only ask this question of people I know want to follow the non-trepreneur path.

The Retirement Mindset
What would you do? If you could stop working in your 30s or 40s, all the control in the world would be handed to you. You could simply carry on like before of course, continuing to work, but with

the knowledge that if you really got too hacked off with it all you could walk away. Or you could go part-time and spend more time with your children, on hobbies, travelling.

A common feature we see in the narratives of folks who've followed the full path, is that they don't retire. Some keep working, but most eventually quit their day jobs and shift into an entrepreneur mindset, kicking off small businesses which they enjoy running, selling products they love on the internet, or helping their communities with building or gardening work. Many choose to write about their experiences, putting together blogs and books, which earn money through advertising, royalties or referrals to financial services. Others do voluntary work for local charities.

Julie and I mixed our approaches. We left our corporate jobs and travelled in a motorhome. As we moved around, we enjoyed writing about our experiences in blog posts and eventually in books, earning a modest but gradually increasing amount of money in the process. After a couple of years, I found my personal progress was slowing down. During this time, I found it difficult to describe myself as *retired*, as it implies a kind of stagnation, and human happiness relies on avoiding that sensation. We need to feel progress to be content, and anyone aiming for early financial independence needs to keep in mind the fact they'll need to steadily find new ways to personally progress as the years pass. For me that involved focussing on physical fitness and writing books, both of which I very much enjoy.

The Work Mindset
The non-trepreneur approach to freedom uses income from your day job to build investments which eventually generate enough money to fund your expenses. Clearly, the bigger the level of income you can generate from your day job, the bigger the opportunity to save and invest. But how do you increase your salary?

If you're lucky enough to be at the very start of your working life, or can switch careers, you can deliberately target higher-income roles. According to the ONS, one of the highest paying jobs in the UK is air traffic controller, with a median average income of £94,431[22]. You'll need a minimum of five GCSEs to get in at entry level, there is no need for a degree[23]. Train and tram drivers come close to the top too, with average incomes of £56,591. This job requires a minimum of two GCSEs (maths and English), again no degree is needed[24]. I've worked alongside freelance IT project managers with no degree earning more than me. One told me how he'd been running his own landscape gardening business before deciding to get into project management. He'd done a course, read a book and had managed to kick off an IT contracting career. I'd worked in IT for 18 years before I dared trying to go freelance.

You might already be part-way through your working life though and shifting between careers is a big ask. There are still some fundamentals which improved my income, whatever job I was doing. I was never brilliant at my job, I'm no genius. Instead, I tried to do the awkward tasks which others avoided. At times I didn't feel like it, but I attempted to consistently work to the very best of my capability too, whatever I was doing. I noticed that the more I volunteered for work which made me nervous, the more I'd be given increased responsibility and eventually more income. It might have meant taking on a project no-one else wanted to touch or applying to be a team leader of a group in difficulty, especially when I knew it would alter my relationship with my co-workers. I would study during evenings or weekends, gaining qualifications

---

[22] *www.ons.gov.uk/employmentandlabourmarket/peopleinwork/ earningsandworkinghours/bulletins/annualsurveyofhoursandearnings/2019#employee-earnings-data*
[23] *www.nats.aero/careers/trainee-air-traffic-controllers*
[24] *nationalcareers.service.gov.uk/job-profiles/train-driver*

which helped demonstrate my capabilities and open new levels in my career.

As I don't know you, I can't know what you personally need to do. You may be held back by limited opportunities in your work environment, or your personal life. Whatever the challenges are for you, you must find a way around these obstacles, you must get it done (search YouTube for *Art Williams Just Do It* for some motivation).

The Relationship Mindset

From a non-trepreneur perspective, your relationship with your spouse and loved ones is critical to making a success of your path to freedom. You'll need to be open with one another about all aspects of your income, how you spend it, what aspirations you have in life and how you're able to achieve them.

A common trait of non-trepreneurs is to track their spending, often down to the penny (or cent, or whatever currency they're using). This tracking has multiple effects, but only works if everyone able to spend money in the household buys into it and habitually takes part. Unless you're able to sit and talk this through calmly, to understand why everyone's doing it without apportioning blame over any previous spending decisions, then it won't work.

Not only do Julie and I track every penny we spend, we also discuss most non-trivial purchases too. By this I mean any single item which costs more than say £50. It might be the shortest of conversations: "I'm thinking of replacing x" or "I'm looking at getting a y", but other times we find ourselves going back and forth a little more. Sometimes the original 'prospective buyer' talks themselves out of the purchase. Other times we come up with an alternative option (borrow, repair, use an alternative). Without trust, openness and a common goal this wouldn't work, as one or both of us would end up feeling resentful.

The Media & News Mindset

To become a non-trepreneur, it helps massively if you can consume as little media and news as possible. The reason why is simple. You're going to need a clear mind to lay down your life and financial goals and get chasing after them. You'll need to focus on your situation and not get distracted by what's going on in the world at large. You'll need to think positively.

Your mind is a glass, and the media will attempt to fill it with murky water. Don't let it, keep your mind clear and objective. Human nature lends our attention to rare and dramatic events. Despite the fact the daily world consists of billions of overwhelmingly unexciting moments in time, this drama-seeking element in our minds forces the news to focus on the tiny minority of sensational or emotionally charged affairs, attacks and unusual circumstances. The news doesn't fully reflect reality.

Going back to the book *Factfulness*, Hans Rosling has demonstrated that the world is a much better place than almost everyone thinks. The media and activists, in a constant struggle to attract attention, are forced to touch the nerves of human instinct to get us clicking and scrolling. Articles which invoke fear, blame, negativity or urgency all serve to grab at us, drawing us towards them.

> URGENT! THIS BAD THING MIGHT AFFECT YOU!

The result is that we perform worse than chimpanzees on multiple choice questions about the state of the world around us, regardless of our vocation, intelligence, numeracy skills or seniority level. For example, Hans posed this question to his worldwide audiences:

"In the last 20 years, the proportion of the world population living in extreme poverty has: A. almost doubled, B. remained more or less the same, C. almost halved."

If you asked this question of the chimpanzees, they'd get it correct 33% of the time by simply guessing. When asked in the UK (human population), only 9% of respondents got it right. The answer is C, but who can recall news articles about such a huge (albeit slow-moving) positive change? On the other hand, we can all recall articles about famine and war in Africa and the Middle East, or terrorist attacks across the world.

Hans is pragmatic about the role of the news, saying *"it is completely unrealistic and unfair to call for the media to change in this way or that so that it can provide us with a better reflection of reality."* Later in his book he gives an indication of how we could manage this built-in bias in media reporting: *"it is up to us as consumers to learn how to consume the news more fact-fully, and to realise that the news is not very useful for understanding the world"*.

I think of the news like a bright, narrow beam of light. It shines on a tiny area of the world for an instant while something interesting is happening, and then it's gone, flashing across the Earth, hungry for the next moment of short-lived excitement. We need to focus our own attention on what we're doing to improve ourselves and our efforts to build income and generate wealth. While Julie and I were chasing financial independence, we had no TV and spent as little time as possible consuming the news.

The Capability Mindset

In his book *Early Retirement Extreme*, Jacob Lund Fisker makes the case for adopting a multi-skill capability mindset. He uses the term *renaissance man* to describe *"a person who is competent in a wide range of fields, covering intellectual areas as well as the arts, physical fitness and social accomplishments."* His point might be summed up like this: we mostly specialise in our jobs, and outsource anything we think is beyond us, or which we think we don't have time for: such as decorating, ironing, gardening, doing tax returns, managing our wealth, servicing the car and so on. This reduces our ability to find solutions for ourselves and builds our dependence on our jobs to earn money to buy the time of others.

I don't consider myself to be a renaissance man, but I do recognise Jacob's point, and, in some ways, I have strived for this model of thinking. I've sometimes opted to buy specialist tools and take to YouTube to learn the skills needed to have a go at DIY jobs myself, rather than bring in a tradesman. Working alongside Julie, I've tiled and plumbed in bathrooms, tiled kitchen floors, installed laminate floors, repointed walls, painted and wall papered, completed tax returns, rebuilt motorbike and van engines, set up a personal pension, built websites and written books.

Aiming for the 'renaissance man' ideal brings the opportunity to reduce our lifestyle costs and increase our self-confidence. We're also better able to use our creative thinking to handle the great expanse of time we will create if we opt to retire early.

The Risk Mindset

After we'd quit our corporate jobs and were out on the road, I couldn't help but worry that we'd taken a senselessly risky decision. Our jobs were in a multi-national corporate, and we still had the upheaval and unemployment created by the 2008 financial crisis in our minds. Would we be able to get back into that kind of job again, even if we wanted to?

Over the weeks it gradually occurred to me that there had been no risk-free options available to us. If we'd stayed in our jobs, we risked depression and eventual burn out. If we'd changed to another company doing something similar, there was a risk we'd feel just the same way. If we'd found jobs which we liked better we might well have missed out on the adventure of a lifetime, increasingly regretting our 'safe' decision as we aged. There were no risk-free paths, just different risks on each path.

The same goes for investing. I used to think of stock market investing as risky. Much too high a risk for me to get involved in. This highlights another aspect to risk: lack of knowledge. I'd created that risky image in my mind from Hollywood films with traders shouting *BUY!* and *SELL!* Nick Leeson bringing down Barings Bank, Leonardo DiCaprio in *The Wolf of Wall Street* and all that. By picking up books and learning the basics, what a share is, what a dividend is, an ETF, an index, I started to grasp not just what risks were actually involved in owning shares, but what opportunities they created too. Owning shares carries risks (we may end up selling them at a loss), but so does not owning them (we could miss out on passive income and need to stay sat behind our desks into our 60s).

The more I thought, the less I could think of life choices which had a completely risk-free option. Have a think about it. Apart from extreme examples like whether to jump from a plane with or without a parachute, can you think of choices you face which have a 100% safe, guaranteed, no-downsides, perfect path?

By accepting the fact I'm always faced with risk, I find it easier to accept it. I feel less worried about making a mistake. I feel more empowered (once I've done my research) to take the action I (we) need to take to achieve our goals. This way of thinking is touched upon in Susan Jeffer's classic book *Feel the Fear and Do It Anyway*: everyone feels fear, but some people choose to act regardless.

In Summary
While there are inevitably a lot of numbers in this book, percentages and a few graphs, none of them are as important as your mindset. If you can successfully change the way you see yourself and the world around you, your chances of achieving financial independence, or any other big goal, are massively increased.

The Non-Trepreneurs

To enable this change, something will need to drive you. Non-trepreneurs are motivated by different things. Some want to spend more time at home with young children, some want to travel, some want to change careers without risking their family finances, some simply want to spend more time on hobbies or their studies. You'll need to do some serious introspection to decide what's important to you and keep your personal goals in mind as you strive for them.

Part Three: Seven Stages to Freedom

"We all have two choices: We can make a living, or we can design a life."

Jim Rohn, American Author and Motivational Speaker

Having read through the life stories of a fair few non-trepreneurs, it seems reasonable to say there is no 'standard' set of steps folks take to achieve their own version of financial freedom. We're all from varying backgrounds and careers, and our starting position will vary. In our case, we started on the path without any knowledge that early financial independence was possible for us, starting to build our cash engines unconsciously for two decades.

I've put together a series of stages as an idealised non-trepreneuer approach. There are many other ways of breaking the problem down[25], and although I've drawn this as a linear set of stages, one after the other, the chances are you'll find yourself shifting backwards and forwards between them.

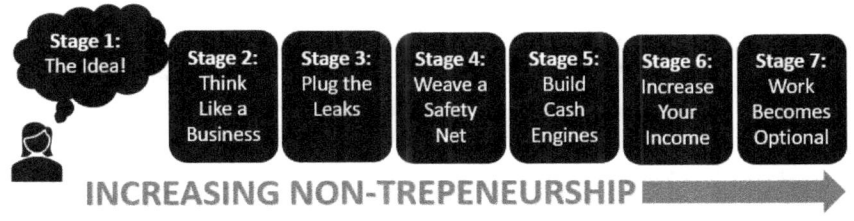

---

[25] For example, see *www.getrichslowly.org/stages-of-financial-freedom*

Stage 1: Get the Idea

Only a small number of individuals get the idea in their heads very early in life, in their teens or 20s, enabling them to mould their careers and lives to meet their eventual goal. While travelling we met a lady who told us how she'd always had an aim to retire to a specific part of the country, a desirable and relatively expensive place to live, and had geared up her career and finances early on to enable it. She had set a savings goal at the start of each year and written it in her diary. She had deliberately moved into a sales position which would enable her to increase her income to meet her aim of buying a series of holiday lets in her dream location.

When we heard her story, we were taken aback: we felt like we'd wasted years drifting without a goal and were equally unnerved and inspired to get started on our own path to freedom.

Like us, most folks don't come across the idea of being able retire early until we're well into our working lives. The idea is a radical one, but it's starting to pop up here and there in the mainstream media. There's even a documentary called *Playing with FIRE* making the rounds[26], albeit in a low-key way. With most of us taking on more and more debt though, those going in the opposite direction are few and far between.

The great news for you is clear: you've obviously been exposed to the idea, through this book if not before. Once the idea that there is an alternative approach to the mainstream work-buy-die life path is lodged in your head, it's very hard to slip backwards.

Stage 2: Think Like a Business

The next stage is to start thinking about your household finances as though you're running a small business. This isn't the same thing as being an entrepreneur. You don't need to come up with an idea

---

[26] *playingwithfire.co/the-documentary*

and you don't need to learn all the skills you need to run a small business: marketing, operations, IT, networking, project management and so on. All you need to do is suss out the accounting part of it, and even that's far simpler for household finances than for a business.

I'll admit this isn't a fun part of the process, but it's crucial. By drawing together the following information about your financial life, you're peeling back the lid on an otherwise opaque, murky box.

The *Household Balance Sheet* (HBS) and *Household Profit & Loss Account* (HPL) we'll create below are like the dashboard and GPS in a car. Without them you can still drive, but it'll be more difficult to get to your destination. The idea isn't just to create these once and then forget about them: they're living documents. We update ours once a month, spending a few minutes checking all is well.

Build a Household Balance Sheet (HBS)

Your HBS will record the value of everything your household owes and owns. By totalling all you own and taking away everything you owe you'll arrive at your household net worth. This will give you some indication how far along the non-trepreneur path you are. Your balance sheet will also make it easy to see the 'things' you own which are creating an income for you, and which are cash flow negative (costing you money).

We use Microsoft Excel for our HBS, but you can use whatever spreadsheet or application you like, or simply a sheet of paper. Creating your balance sheet should be relatively easy. You'll need to get hold of your bank account balances, your latest pension and mortgage statements, and your latest loan and credit card balances. You'll also need to get estimates of the market value of any assets you have, like your house and car (websites like *zoopla.com* and *autotrader.co.uk* should give you good-enough figures).

The Non-Trepreneurs

Here's a sample Household Balance Sheet, just for the purposes of discussion. Ours is more complex than this, but not much more.

Assets

House Market Value	£272,000
Car Combined Value	£10,500
Cash in Current Account	£4,500
Cash in ISAs	£5,600
Cash in Premium Bonds	£1,000
Pension Transfer Value	£28,000

Liabilities

Mortgage	-£213,000
Car Loans	-£2,100
Credit Card Balance	-£1,000

Net Worth: £105,500

We can make some observations from this HBS:

- This household has a positive net worth, which is great news, they're on the first steps to freedom! Many will be negative, especially younger folks with student loan debt.
- We can look down the list of assets and work out which:
  - take money from their accounts (the house and car),
  - add money to their accounts (Premium Bonds, although only to a small extent),
  - will add money to their accounts in the future (pension).

  The idea is to get as much money into the latter two types of asset, cash-generating assets which will create passive income in future.
- There are no significant cash-generating assets listed. No rental properties, no stocks, no bond funds. Yes, there is cash and Premium Bonds, but interest and 'winnings' income is likely to be negligible.

Part Three: Seven Stages to Freedom

- The pension is starting to build up, but it won't generate any income until at least age 55. Using the 4% Safe Withdrawal Rate (SWR) described on page 133, a £28,000 pension will create roughly 28,000 x (4 ÷ 100) = £1,120 annual retirement income before-tax.
- There's significant debt: a mortgage, car loans and credit card(s). It should go without saying the credit card debt MUST be paid off in full each month, which it probably is here as the balance is relatively low and there is cash available. The car loan is a worry as it shows a mindset where taking on expensive debt is acceptable. The mortgage will have the lowest interest rate of them all, and it's debateable whether there's a need to focus on paying it off before investing.

To give you an idea of what the Household Balance Sheet of a financially-free household might look like, here's one I've made up:

Assets

House Value	£172,000
Car Value	£3,500
Cash in Current Account	£4,500
Cash in Premium Bonds	£40,000
Rental Flat	£150,000
Stocks & Shares ISAs	£308,000
Pension Transfer Value	£288,000

Liabilities

Credit Card Balance	-£500

Net Worth: £965,500

Some observations from this second HBS:
- The house value is lower, perhaps these non-trepreneurs moved to a lower cost area or downsized. There's no mortgage or car loan: they've been paid off (or not taken out).

- The net worth is close to £1m. Of this, the main cash-generating assets are held in stocks & shares ISAs. This might be invested in low cost, passive index tracker funds (shares), creating roughly £12,000 of income each year at a 4% SWR (£308,000 x (4 ÷ 100) = £12,320).
- The household owns a paid off rental flat which, after all costs, creates an income of £6,000 a year (assuming a 4% after-costs return on £150,000).
- If the £18,000 income from the shares and the rental flat exceeds this household's yearly costs (possible for a frugal couple with no mortgage), then they are financially-free at this point and can stop working if they wish.
- Alternatively, they could opt to rent their house out and travel, generating an additional £6,000 in income while they're away.
- The £288,000 pension fund might generate roughly £11,000 a year once it becomes accessible (again working at a 4% SWR), taking the total household pre-tax passive income to £29,000 a year (or £35,000 if the house is being rented out too).
- The household has a significant amount held in cash-like Premium Bonds, maybe enough to cover 18 months to two year's living expenses. These generate a low income (perhaps 1% a year, which is likely less than inflation), but act as a sleep-at-night fund, also known as an emergency fund. By having such a large amount available, a financial shock like a tenant stopping paying rent or a long-term stock market crash shouldn't be a major problem in the event this couple did opt to leave work.

If you're thinking 'how on earth are we supposed to get that amount of money together' you're not alone. Everyone has this question, and the answer to it will depend very much on your personal circumstances, your ability to increase your income, your goal-setting capabilities, what options you have to streamline your spending (in ways which might currently be hidden to you) and

Part Three: Seven Stages to Freedom

how willing you are to build your financial knowledge and take the risks involved in investing. The rest of this book is dedicated to helping you build the knowledge, attitude, discipline and resources needed to bulk up your balance sheet to the point you're eventually financially free.

Build a Household Profit & Loss Account (HPL)

The other information sheet you need to build will record where your income comes from, and where it all goes. This is your Household Profit & Loss account or HPL, and despite how dry and dull it might sound, it's a pure, thoroughbred racehorse when it comes to delivering you from servitude!

Creating and maintaining a HPL takes long-term focus and energy, although there are lots of budgeting and cost-tracking apps available now which should make the task far simpler. In our case Julie tracks our costs manually, having gotten into the habit before the apps were available. See page 97 for practical information on how we go about tracking our household costs. Whichever method you use to maintain it, your HPL is absolutely, 100% critical to getting financially strong.

You need your own HPL to know your numbers, how much you spend each month and year and what on. I can't stress this enough, you MUST create and maintain a HPL or your chances of getting free early in life are frankly miniscule. To go back to the car analogy I used earlier, if your HBS is your dashboard, not having a HPL would be like driving without your satnav, in the dark with your lights off, while wearing sunglasses. You're driving blind.

Here's an invented household's HPL to give us a simple example to work through. In this example, all figures are annual, so we can capture one-off costs like insurance premiums which we might miss if we just focussed on a single month. In practice Julie and I have a monthly HPL, and we don't bother using more advanced accounting concepts to spread out the costs (accruals and pre-

The Non-Trepreneurs

payments). Instead, we just keep in mind some months will have higher costs than others. With several years of HPL to look back on, we know when those months are and have a very good idea of how much the annual costs will be when they come.

Annual Income

After Tax Wage 1	£25,000
After Tax Wage 2	£32,000
Premium Bonds	£250
Total Income:	**£57,250**

Annual Outgoings

Mortgage	-£13,380
Supermarket	-£5,200
Eating Out/Takeaways	-£2,400
TV Subscription	-£600
Cars Insurance/Breakdown	-£868
Car Loan	-£2,604
Cars Service, MOT, Repairs	-£878
Cars Fuel	-£4,389
House Insurance	-£230
Gas, Electricity & Internet	-£1450
Water	-£160
Mobile Phones	-£720
Council Tax	-£1,458
Pension Contributions	-£2,600
Clothes	-£1,560
Going Out/Having Fun	-£3,500
Presents	-£1,200
Magazine Subscriptions	-£48
Holidays	-£2,600
Miscellaneous	-£2,400
Total Expenses:	**-£48,245**

Income less Expenses: £9,005

Part Three: Seven Stages to Freedom

Let's see what observations we can draw from this example HPL:

- This household appears to be DINKYs (dual income, no kids yet). This explains the lack of childcare and other similar costs.
- The household is generating around £9,000 a year more than they're spending – good news!
- They're almost entirely wage-dependant, with only a small amount of premium bond income alongside their salaries.
- They appear to have two cars, and have significant commutes looking at the fuel cost.
- They're contributing roughly 5% a year into their pensions. If they're lucky their employers might contribute the same, pushing their savings rate up to 10%. They're looking at a 50+ year working life at this rate.
- Their 'miscellaneous' costs of £2,400 represent a big savings possibility. What's in here? What can they remove from this generic bucket?

The purpose of the HPL is two-fold:

1. To enable you to **discover where your money is going**, and in turn to plug the cash leaks, lower your expenses and make sure you're consistently saving much more than you earn.
2. To let you **see where your income is coming from**. As your cash-generating investments increase they'll gradually get closer to your expenses until they inevitably meet all your needs. You can graph this out, like in the example below.

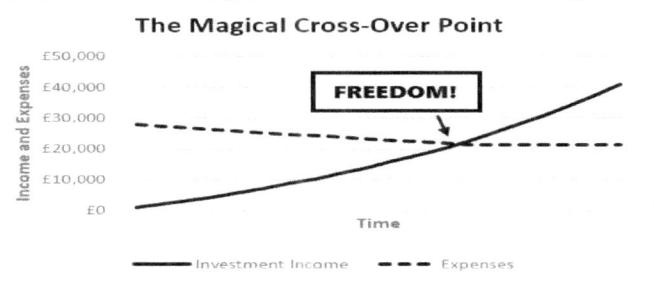

The Non-Trepreneurs

In the graph we've assumed your expenses will gradually fall then bottom out as you get better at spotting cash leaks and removing them. Where your investment income equals your expenses, you've reached the magical cross-over point from being dependant on your salary to being financially-free, and congratulations are in order!

Build a Dashboard

Julie updates our HBS once a month, and our HPL every few days. From these two data sources she's been able to put together an auto-updated sheet of graphs which we call our dashboard. It has the following graphs on it:

- **Monthly Spend and Income** – this shows whether we spent more or less than our income each month, and how much the difference was. We use this for an 'at a glance' idea of whether we're spending too much, or too little.
- **Cash and Premium Bonds Value** – this tracks how much we have in our cash accounts, our cash ISAs and our Premium Bonds. Together these make up our emergency fund, and we use the graph to keep an eye on whether we're depleting it, or whether it's growing too much, and we need to take money from it and invest it in share funds.
- **Shares Value** – this adds together the value of our stocks and shares ISAs, enabling us to see whether short-term stock market fluctuations are affecting our net worth and overall liquid asset value.
- **All Liquid Assets** – this adds the value of our shares to the emergency fund. Effectively this is the amount we have in case things go really, badly, terribly wrong. If forced to, we could sell our shares quickly. Added to our emergency fund, this would release around a decade's worth of living costs.
- **Net Worth** – this simply shows how our net worth is changing over time. It's not that useful to be honest, it's more for our egos than anything else.

We review the dashboard each month for a few minutes, and if we spot anything weird happening dive into the numbers to have a look. It gives us an at-a-glance overview of our current financial position in just the way we want it presented.

Build a Budget

Businesses tend to constrain their costs using budgets. They allocate a certain amount each year to spending on various categories: £x on rent, £y on advertising and so on. Lots of personal finance gurus propose a similar approach for managing household finances. We don't have any arguments against this approach, but we don't do it ourselves.

While we have an overall sum we plan to spend each year, we don't allocate amounts to our HPL categories. For example, we've never had a pre-defined amount we plan to spend on sports equipment, fuel for our motorhome, home insurance or supermarket shopping. Why not? We've never needed to do this to keep within our yearly budget. We do 'drill down' into our costs during monthly reviews to see where any bigger-than-usual expenses have caused a spike in spending. Our yearly budget is currently £20,000, which includes all our day-to-day living costs, but not costs related to our house rentals or our partnership, such as management fees, repairs, mortgage interest, insurance, accountant fees and so on. We divide our yearly budget into a weekly amount and keep a running account of how much we've spent in the year-to-date, to avoid any surprises at the end of the year.

Once you have a HPL, you can of course choose to define a budget for each of your categories, if that approach works for your household. If you have difficult trade-offs to make, having a pre-defined budget for each category might keep you on track when the tough decisions arise.

Stage 3: Plug the Leaks

Now we have figures to inform our thinking, we can move onto the next stage, which is to really focus on what's critical. Using the example HPL above, this household appears to be in a good financial position. Assuming they maintain (or improve) their dual salaries and manage to improve the rate at which they're contributing to their pensions, a comfortable retirement in their 60s looks entirely possible.

But that's not what this book is about. This is a book about removing the need to work much, much earlier, and doing it by saving and investing income from a job. With this in mind, let's have another look at the hypothetical couple above.

They have a combined after-tax income of £57,250. This places them in a good position to achieve financial freedom. If they can refine their expenses down to £29,000, they can potentially save and invest 50% of their income, drastically reducing their working lives from 50+ years all the way down to less than 20 years[27].

This household has two opportunities available to them:

- They can generate more income, by changing jobs, self-educating themselves, working overtime, starting to invest, starting side gigs and so on.
- They can modify their mindset around spending, allowing them to save and invest more of their income.

Ideally, they will do a bit of both, but it's this second point we're looking at here. What opportunities are there for this household to save significantly more of their money? On the face of it, there may not be any. Other than their pension contributions, they're spending

---

[27] *networthify.com/calculator/earlyretirement*

Part Three: Seven Stages to Freedom

almost everything they earn, but have they considered opportunities such as:

- **Re-mortgaging to a lower cost deal.** On a £213,000, 25-year term mortgage, a 1% interest rate reduction from 3.5% to 2.5% would save them £33,000 in interest[28] over the life of the loan.
- **Renting out a bedroom to a lodger.** Sites like *spareroom.com* will give you an idea of potential income, and this couple could earn up to £7,200 a year tax-free under the Rent a Room scheme[29].
- **Moving close to work and selling one or both cars.** We often underestimate the cost of commuting. A £8,500 Vauxhall Astra might cost £3,500 a year to run[30]. A £12,000 Nissan Qashqai comes in at around £5,800 a year.
- **Reducing their TV package, shifting to free TV or selling the TV.** There's a potential £600 a year (£6,000 a decade) saving here, based on cancelling a £50-a-month subscription, but perhaps the biggest advantage of this change isn't cost, but the time freed up to do more useful stuff: to run a side business, to read and self-educate, to exercise and so on.
- **Changing their mindset around reward and fun.** They could reduce their eating out to once a month, finding free things to do and places to go instead. The couple is currently spending around £5,900 a year on eating and going out. With some changes in habits there's a potential saving of maybe £30,000 a decade.
- **Focussing in on small-cost habits.** Someone drinking a single pint of beer a day at £4 a pint, will get through almost £15,000 a decade. Someone smoking 20 cigarettes a day will burn

---

[28] *www.moneysavingexpert.com/mortgages/mortgage-rate-calculator*
[29] *www.gov.uk/rent-room-in-your-home/the-rent-a-room-scheme*
[30] *www.moneyadviceservice.org.uk/en/tools/car-costs-calculator*

through £40,000 every ten years. That's in real terms, more if you allow for inflation.

Paying Yourself First

The *pay yourself first* approach is a psychological trick, which hides a chunk of your income, so you don't see it as available for discretionary spending. It's very simple. Each month you automatically move a chunk of your income into investments or a savings account before paying your bills. Of course, it relies on your income exceeding your essential outgoings each month, you must keep paying your mortgage and utility bills!

We used this approach for two decades to build up occupational pensions. Our employer's payroll departments deducted money from our salaries and placed it in our pensions before paying us. We never saw it in our bank accounts, so never spent it. We didn't even miss it. We did something similar while paying our mortgage down, manually over-paying our mortgage as soon as our salaries arrived each month, leaving enough in our account for our costs.

Stage 4: Weave a Safety Net

When I started writing this, we were three months into the 2020 COVID-19 pandemic lockdown here in the UK. Almost as soon as the virus hit the United States, video clips started to appear on news sites, showing huge lines of cars waiting to collect food parcels. In one of the richest nations on Earth, thousands of unfortunate people were forced into food poverty the moment they lost their incomes, as they had no savings to fall back on.

Here in the UK I see adverts for payday loans on the TV. They typically depict a panicked parent, faced with an unexpected cost like a car or washing machine breakdown. The loans are offered by around 90 different lenders, and consumers borrow around £1.3 billion a year. They repay over £2 billion. That's £700 million in interest payments[31], ouch! Why? Because the borrowers being preyed upon have no savings and aren't going to be able to build them while they're paying so much back in interest.

In my opinion, before thinking about starting to invest, it makes sense to get yourself into a safe and secure financial position. In other words:

- Save up enough money to cover 3 to 6 months of living expenses (if you spend £40,000 a year, save up £10,000 to £20,000). Place it into a savings account (or Premium Bonds) and don't touch it, ever, unless it's a genuine emergency. This is your emergency fund, and it's going to be your friend, comforter and lifeguard throughout your life.
- Make sure you're appropriately insured. If your jobs don't provide 'death in service' cover, you might want to buy life insurance, to ensure the surviving partner or dependants can cover the bills in the event one of you dies. Again, if your jobs don't provide cover for it, critical illness cover will enable you to pay the bills in the event one of you is unable to work.

Stage 5: Build Cash Engines

You must invest in cash-generating assets in order to retire early. Trying to do it by just saving cash in a current or savings account is nigh-on impossible, you'd need huge amounts of money. We've only a set number of years to accumulate the assets we need, maybe two or three decades. At the point we feel we have enough investments, we can retire and use those assets to fund our retirements, this is the 'glide path'.

I've illustrated this in the following graph, but in a highly theoretical way, the lines will never be this smooth! There's also a

---

[31] *www.fca.org.uk/data/consumer-credit-high-cost-short-term-credit-lending-data-jan-2019*

The Non-Trepreneurs

real possibility of our net worth increasing in retirement, if we continue to earn more than we spend and invest well, so the glide path could continue upwards.

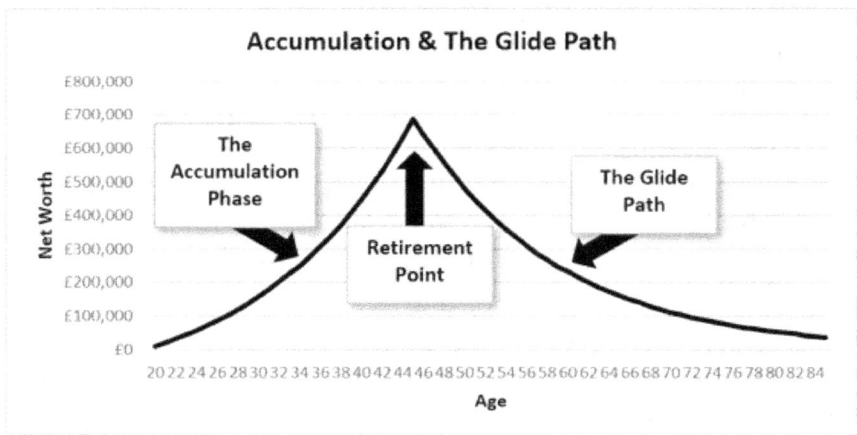

Inflation's a big problem and anyone wanting to retire early must set up their finances to account for it during the glide path. Something which costs £1 today will more than quadruple in cost in 50 years' time (if inflation averages 3% a year). Applied to all our costs equally, we'd need to ensure our income also increases by a factor of four over the same time period, to be sure we can retain the same living standard. If we spend £25,000 a year today, we'll need £100,000 a year in 50 years' time.

If you retire at 40 you might conceivably live another 50 years. Even with a relatively conservative yearly spend of £25,000, increasing at 3% a year (in line with inflation), you'd need £2.8m saved in a 0% interest cash savings account before you quit work (assuming no state pension or other forms of income). You can do your own sums, working out each year's costs as follows:

- Year 1 = £25,000.00
- Year 2 = £25,000.00 × 1.03 = £25,750.00
- Year 3 = £25,750.00 × 1.03 = £26,522.50

- Year 4 = £26,522.50 x 1.03 = £27,318.18
- And so on, finally adding together all the yearly costs to get £2,819,921.

If you could get 3% interest on your cash, you'd need far less, but still £1.23m. On the other hand, if you can buy share and bond funds which return a long-term average of 7% a year, then your target investment amount is reduced to £625,000 (see page 133), still a lot of money, but a far more palatable amount.

Cash-generating investments don't just support us better during the glide path after our main earning years, they also enable us to get to our target amount faster. As soon as you've got your first £1,000 into an investment which is increasing at 7% a year, those £££s will start to slowly multiply. I think of this as the opposite of the terrifying spiralling debt I sometimes read about where some unfortunate individuals are trapped in increasing debt. Instead of you owing more and more as interest is charged on interest, your investments earn more and more, like spiralling wealth machines.

A big challenge here for most of us (aside from finding the money to invest in the first place), is understanding what kinds of personal investment are appropriate to us. How do they work? What risks do we face? What level of research do we need to do? What kinds of behaviour do we exhibit? How do we avoid problems with tax or other legal implications? What kinds of realistic returns might we make? What records do we need to keep? We'll come onto this in Part Six: Building Cash Engines on page 112.

Stage 6: Increasing Your Income

If you're able to increase your income without succumbing to lifestyle inflation (spending more), then you'll accelerate the rate at which you can build your cash engines, it's that simple. There are a few areas to investigate when you're thinking about this stage:

Building Your Value

Julie and I developed high-value, transferable corporate skills over our careers, project management, budgeting, team leading, presentation skills, risk management, consulting, networking and stakeholder management, for example. Coupled with industry knowledge, we could command good salaries, but they didn't just happen like magic, they took work, effort and thought.

We both found that we'd get bored in a job after a few years and would change company in search of something more challenging, which often came with an associated pay rise. When we started working for a multi-national corporation, there was much more opportunity to move within the company, again increasing our responsibility and salary, but without the hassle of starting over at a new workplace.

Often changing jobs required new skills. Sometimes we could make the case for our employer to pay for the training needed, and other times we trained ourselves, buying books, online courses, equipment or taking evening classes. Sometimes the skills came from doing the work. Learning to manage people was one of those times, where the company assumed (wrongly in my case) that someone with technical skills could simply shift into team management. Being a leader, understanding what fears, talents and motivations your staff have, is a completely different job to understanding technical concepts.

Other times, we found we could make ourselves more valuable by simply being the best we could be. Although not always successful, we tried to be positive, to present solutions alongside challenges, to do each job to the best of our ability, to volunteer for jobs others didn't want to do, to think around issues. Eventually all of this paid off when new positions came available and we had the opportunity to interview for them. Getting a mentor was very helpful too, someone successful in the organisation who's willing to give you some of their time to help you understand what kinds of things you need to do to progress.

Going It Alone

I worked in Corporate IT, where a small army of temporary contractors were used. Sometimes they were employed for specialist skills, and other times to allow the organisation to deliver labour-intensive projects which it didn't have the full-time manpower to handle.

The temps were all self-employed on short-term contracts, working for their own limited companies. They were paid a daily rate, plus travel expenses, and it was their own responsibility to arrange for their own pensions, training, sickness/maternity/holiday pay, national insurance and public liability insurance. They also had to ensure their companies submitted accounts to HMRC, and that they operated with the prevailing tax law.

The main upside for contractors was increased income. I did the exact same tasks that I had as a full-time employee and used the exact same skills. But after I switched to contracting, I roughly doubled my take home pay. Admittedly, this was partly because I took few holidays when I knew each day off would cost me hundreds of pounds.

Interestingly, the corporate culture pressurised full-time employees to work more hours than they were paid for, to be contactable on holiday and so on. None of this was applied to contractors, perhaps because the organisation knew they'd be billed if they tried it. Working as a contractor was less stressful for me as a result. I also avoided other elements of corporate culture which I didn't enjoy, like team building away days.

I know not everyone can go it alone, and not everyone would have it as easy in terms of finding work (I only had three clients, and they all paid on time). If shifting into self-employment is an option for you though, it's worth at least thinking about, especially when your cash engines are up and running and already feeding in some income, taking the pressure off you.

Side Hustles
Side hustles/gigs are a big thing in the FIRE blogging community. They're a new word for moonlighting, running a second or even third job alongside the day job. As our day jobs generated very good incomes for us, it made more sense for us personally to focus on them rather than side gigs. However, we have done a few of them in between working or in retirement, including blogging, pet sitting, self-publishing books and working as a Utility Warehouse distributor (*www.julieandjay.co.uk*).

Other side gigs include offering childcare (if you're a stay-at-home parent), pet walking, running evening/out-of-school classes, being a virtual assistant or just getting a job stacking shelves/serving coffee and so on.

Negotiating Payoffs
This is a one-off cash generation opportunity rather than an income increasing strategy, but it's worth thinking about. A few times in my career my employer laid people off. At the time I didn't want to be made redundant, and couldn't afford it either, so it was a time of stress, not opportunity (I didn't always have an emergency fund, more fool me!).

If I could have planned my exit from each organisation I worked for, I might have been able to negotiate a payoff from my employers. Given the same opportunity again, instead of simply handing my notice in I'd have done research and thought whether I could engineer my own redundancy, without burning my bridges.

Stage 7: Work Becomes Optional
Eventually, income from your investments equals your ongoing expenses. This is the tipping point. Once you're here, your day job

is no longer mandatory. If you choose to, you can retire and never work another day in your life. This is quite an incredible place to be, I can assure you. I found it somewhat bewildering too. Despite the fact we'd planned and worked hard for it, the fact we appeared to have succeeded took years to really sink in.

The reality is this point is always going to be a fuzzy one, a grey area, an act of faith to a degree. No matter how well we track our expenses today, forecast what inflation might be and make estimates of tax bills, we can't be sure what our real costs will be decades from now. There is no guarantee how well our investments will perform either. They could systematically underperform our expectations years after leaving our careers, placing us in a position where we're unable to slot back into our old working lives.

There are a few ways Julie and I manage this potential situation:

- We think of our lives as an experiment: we know this might not work, and we're open to doing relatively low-paid jobs if needs be to bolster our finances.
- We've become small-scale entrepreneurs, generating additional cash which enables us to continue to save and invest 20% of our income.
- We've continued detailed cost and income tracking, which enables us to keep a casual but close eye on what our finances are doing.

Many folks reach the tipping point and find themselves succumbing to *one-more-year syndrome*. This is driven by fear. They continue to work jobs they don't like, as they're fearful their calculations aren't correct. The risk here is a simple one: there's no getting those years back. Once they're gone, they're gone. As ever, we can always find a way to earn more money, but we can't go back in time and regain a year of life.

The Non-Trepreneurs

In the online FIRE blogging world, several classifications of people's financial situation 'in retirement' have been created. There is no consensus over who fits into which category, what categories there should be, or what they should be called, but we'll pop in some rough numbers to give an idea how this works. All the income figures are for a household, rather than an individual.

- **Fat FIRE** – these are households who don't consider themselves frugal. Physician on Fire (*physicianonfire.com*) defines households which are Fat FIRE[32] as having investments which generate double the average household spend. For the UK that will be around £70,000 a year, requiring cash-generating assets of roughly £1.75m to £2.3m.
- **Standard FIRE** – these might be defined as households with passive incomes roughly around the national median average in the UK, which is around £30,000 plus council and income tax, so let's say roughly £35,000. This requires investments totalling around £875,000 to £1.2m.
- **Lean FIRE** – these are the more frugal households, living in lower cost-of-living areas in smaller properties and taking a more minimalist approach to life. Income at this level could be down to less than £10,000 a year for those living in motorhomes or narrowboats full-time, for example, but I'll place Lean FIRE income at around £25,000, requiring £625,000 to £825,000 in investments.
- **Barista FIRE** – this is early retirement in which you opt to bolster your income with low-stress jobs from time to time. You've a large investment portfolio behind you providing significant retirement income, say £500,000 creating maybe £20,000 a year. You might earn another £5,000 a year through working.

---

[32] *www.physicianonfire.com/fatfire*

Julie and I are currently in the Lean FIRE category (although we're a little Barista FIRE too, and once we can access our pensions we'll shift towards Standard FIRE). We spend our lives living in small spaces which many people would find cramped and uncomfortable, but it works well for us. We think of people living on narrowboats or apartments in cities, who often have less space than us. We're very careful around what we spend our money on, repairing and re-using as and when we can. We're happy to DIY but use professionals for maintaining our rental properties.

When I read about FIRE bloggers with £2m, £3m, £4m or more in investments, I freely admit to feeling a degree of fear, uncertainty and jealousy. Have we quit too early? Have we overly-constrained our lives by opting to live on a relatively small income? Are we wrong being so frugal? Would our lives be improved if we'd spent another decade at work? I don't have the answers to these questions, other than to say neither of us regret the actions we've taken. There's a clear tension between Thin FIRE and Fat FIRE advocates on the internet. The former portrays the latter as wasteful, while Fat FIRE advocates say living on Thin FIRE incomes is either not possible (they're really Barista FIRE, or one partner is still working) or is a life of deprivation.

I try to take a step backwards and look at myself. I'm 48 and have been retired from work for five years. I've done a few months of work here and there, but not a great deal. I'm in good health, able to run 40 or 50 miles a week. I have a great relationship with my wife. I can travel freely across Europe in our motorhome, usually for months at a time. In the real world, outside the world of FIRE blogs, I'm a seriously rich man. My feeling is most people on Earth, especially those outside the comfort and security of 'the West' would be very happy living my life, regardless of what 'level' of FIRE I am. I know that I am.

The Non-Trepreneurs

In Summary

There is no set path to achieving financial independence. Even excluding the business-building approaches entrepreneurs take, us non-trepreneurs have a whole range of paths available. Few people's path will be smooth and those opting to take the non-trepreneur approach will do so at different points in their lives.

Everyone must find their own path, but there's no harm in pulling together a theoretical set of stages, as we have in this part of the book. The key elements for most of us will be similar:

- tracking our income and spending,
- assessing and redesigning our lives to get our costs and income into the right place to support our goals,
- and learning to invest and taking action to build cash-generating assets.

Eventually this approach will enable an early escape from the workforce, if that's your aim.

Part Four: An Efficiently Spent Life

"Spending money is a failure to solve problems by smarter means."

Jacob Lund Fisker, Author of *Early Retirement Extreme*

How much money do we need to spend to be content and comfortable? If we take our cues from the media and society around us, the answer is what we earn, if not more. If we do this, then we're quietly agreeing to a 50 or 60 year enforced working life, but the media tells us the alternative is a life of deprivation. Who's correct?

An Average Financial Life

What do we earn over our lifetimes, and where does all our income go? Playing an average UK couple's financial life on fast-forwards, it might go something like this:

- They head to university at 18 (50% of school leavers now go to university[33]) and leave with student loan debt of £36,000[34].
- They start their first jobs on £24,000 a year[35].
- They buy (or lease) their first car by the time they're 26[36], spending £9,000 on their first year's motoring costs[37].
- If they live near us, they'll buy their first home around age 32, spending £190,000 on a three-bed semi-detached house[38].

---

[33] *www.telegraph.co.uk/news/2019/09/26/half-young-people-going-university-first-time-figures-reveal*
[34] *commonslibrary.parliament.uk/research-briefings/sn01079*
[35] *www.graduate-jobs.com/gco/Booklet/graduate-salary-salaries.jsp*
[36] *www.thisismoney.co.uk/money/cars/article-3698959/Are-young-people-priced-driving-Average-age-drivers-taking-test.html*
[37] *www.motoringresearch.com/car-news/young-drivers-first-year-cost*
[38] *www.zoopla.co.uk/discover/first-time-buyers/first-time-buyers-zoopla*

The Non-Trepreneurs

- They'll need a household income of £42,250 to buy the house. Their mortgage will last 29 years and cost them £100,000 in interest (at 3.5% interest on a £170,000 loan[39]).
- Around the same time, they have their first of 1.9 children[40], and get married too[41] spending £27,161 on the big day[42].
- They'll contribute to personal pensions during their 20s (38% of men and women) or 30s (57% of men and 51% of women)[43].
- They take their second step on the housing ladder aged 42, spending £75,000 more on their next home[44].
- Their earnings peak in their 40s before steadily declining[45].
- Over their entire working life, they earn £2.1m between them[46].
- They'll retire when they're around 65, with roughly 50% of their income coming from private pensions, the other 50% from the state pension[47].

---

[39] *www.moneysavingexpert.com/mortgages/mortgage-rate-calculator*
[40] *www.ons.gov.uk/peoplepopulationandcommunity/birthsdeathsandmarriages/livebirths/bulletins/birthcharacteristicsinenglandandwales/2018*
[41] *www.ons.gov.uk/peoplepopulationandcommunity/birthsdeathsandmarriages/marriagecohabitationandcivilpartnerships/bulletins/marriagesinenglandandwalesprovisional/2017*
[42] *www.moneyadviceservice.org.uk/blog/how-much-does-an-average-wedding-cost*
[43] *www.pensionspolicyinstitute.org.uk/media/3506/20200610-ppi-pension-facts-final.pdf*
[44] *www.independent.co.uk/news/property-ladder-age-average-house-price-millennial-first-time-buyers-baby-boomer-retired-a8907281.html*
[45] *www.ons.gov.uk/employmentandlabourmarket/peopleinwork/earningsandworkinghours/bulletins/annualsurveyofhoursandearnings/2019*
[46] *www.ons.gov.uk/peoplepopulationandcommunity/wellbeing/articles/humancapitalestimates/2004to2018*
[47] *www.pensionspolicyinstitute.org.uk/media/3506/20200610-ppi-pension-facts-final.pdf*

Of course, there is no such thing as 'the average couple', but the figures offer us some interesting insights, the biggest of which is how large some of the sums of money are.

Given how much we (on average) spend on getting married, buying bigger homes, bringing up children and driving, there's surely some opportunity for many of us to make big savings in our lives?

We've already noted that seemingly small, habit-driven, repeating costs like a £4 pint of beer add up to huge amounts of money (£15,000 over a decade) over long periods of time. There are many other huge inherent costs in many of our lives which we simply take for granted. If we can re-engineer our lifestyles, we could bring forwards our financial independence by years, if not decades.

The Compounding Effect of Saving

Avoiding spending is far more exciting for me when I consider what I can do with the money instead, or what it can do for me. By thinking of saving in terms of how it can help build investments, I'm far more motivated to avoid unnecessary costs. Let's have a quick look at a single example of how repeated, relatively small savings can have an enormous affect over time.

Let's assume you can find a way to save £42 a month. Maybe you call your television company and cancel your subscription, watching FreeView instead. Perhaps you no longer really need that magazine subscription you've had for years? Maybe you can cut back by three pints of beer a week? However you find the money, saving £42 a month is the equivalent of a £500 a year savings habit.

Let's also assume you can increase your £500 saving by 3% each year, keeping up with inflation, so in the second year you can save £515, the third £530 and so on. The following table shows, even in a 0% interest savings account, over a 40-year period this single change will turn into over £37,000.

The Non-Trepreneurs

Year	Saved per Year	Total Saved
1	£500	£500
2	£515	£1,015
3	£530	£1,545
4	£546	£2,092
5	£563	£2,655
...	...	...
10	£652	£5,732
20	£877	£13,435
30	£1,178	£23,788
40	£1,584	£37,701

However, the true opportunity of saving is to invest the saved money. £37,000 is nice, but would you rather have £146,000?

Let's now assume that instead of keeping our £42 a month in a zero-interest account, we place the money in stock market funds, in an ISA or personal pension, where we might expect a realistic average return of 7% a year over the long term. The table below shows what happens (in theory, in practice the line would never be this smooth as the market return fluctuates).

Year	Saved per Year	Investment Return @ 7%	Total Invested
1	£500	£0	£500
2	£515	£35	£1,050
3	£530	£74	£1,654
4	£546	£116	£2,316
5	£563	£162	£3,041
...	...	...	...
10	£652	£467	£7,790
20	£877	£1,630	£25,795
30	£1,178	£4,163	£64,812
40	£1,584	£9,474	£146,405

Part Four: An Efficiently Spent Life

Putting the table in a graph and you can clearly see how the total wealth from the £42 a month savings habit accelerates upwards over the years:

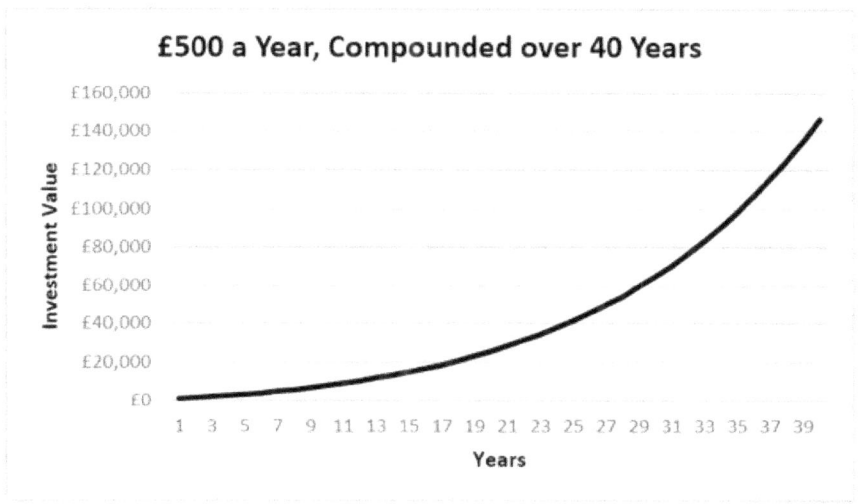

This is the compound effect, the way in which you earn 'interest on interest', which accelerates your wealth line upwards like a fighter aircraft taking off. It's an incredibly exciting concept, but it only works if you're able to think and behave long-term. The effect takes decades to really crank your wealth upwards.

I should point out that the sum of £146,405 in 40 years' time will have the same purchasing power as £44,881 in today's money (at 3% average inflation), almost four times as much as if you had left it in a zero-interest savings account (£37,701 would be worth £11,557 in today's money). A single £42-a-month saving habit could be turned into almost £45,000 in real wealth. It's like a kind of magic.

OK, that's just a small example. Let's shift up a gear now and get started with the big costs in our lives. The bigger the costs, the bigger the opportunity to save, and the more exciting the opportunity for investing those savings. Lifestyle changes in these areas might easily translate into hitting financial independence years or even decades earlier than the norm.

The Big Five Costs

If we dig into the average family's spending, five categories rise to the top of the pile, let's cast a non-trepreneurial eye over each of them:

- housing,
- transport,
- recreation & culture,
- food,
- children.

Big Cost One: Housing

Mortgage interest, council tax, utility bills, maintenance and home improvements make housing our number one cost here in the UK. Of course, we need somewhere to live, so how can we think about housing costs as anything other than mandatory?

There is, of course, the option of not living in a house. This is most-likely appropriate to couples or those with smaller children. Advocates of 'alternative living' choose lower-cost options like narrowboats, motorhomes and caravans. Julie and I have lived in a 6m long motorhome for over four years, on and off over the past decade. The day-to-day costs compared to bricks-n-mortar are vastly reduced, especially if you can take to the continent with its network of free or low-cost overnight parking options.

However, boats and vans tend to depreciate, while houses tend to appreciate over the long term. We worked this out when thinking about living on a narrowboat (a £200,000 house appreciating at 2% a year will be worth almost £40,000 more after a decade, while a boat would likely lose value). Also, these options are only ever going to appeal to a small percentage of the population and might prove impractical as we age.

Part Four: An Efficiently Spent Life

Returning to traditional housing, how else can we think about how we spend money on our home? Let's get started with spare rooms. According to the Independent[48], there are at least 18.6 million spare rooms in the UK's 30 million dwellings. In the UK these are the average current house prices (from *zoopla.co.uk*), along with the amount of interest you'd pay on a 25-year 80% repayment mortgage at 3.5%:

Bedrooms	Price	Interest	Interest Per Additional Bedroom
1 Bed	£208,681	£83,871	-
2 Bed	£239,634	£96,311	£12,440
3 Bed	£325,397	£130,779	£34,468
4 Bed	£540,423	£217,201	£86,422
5 Bed	£932,025	£374,589	£157,388

Even ignoring the council tax, decoration, furnishings, insurance and heating, if you buy a 3-bed house to get a single spare bedroom, that room will cost on average £34,468, or £1,379 a year in interest payments compared with an average 2-bed house. That's a lot of money for a room you might hardly use.

Remember though, it's not just about the cost saving, £1,379 per year invested with an annual return of 7%, would be worth £87,220 at the end of the 25-year mortgage term. If left for another 15 years, without investing any more money, that £87,220 could grow to £240,643 by the end the owner's 40-year working life.

If you already have a spare room and don't want to move, you could rent it out to a lodger. Again, I appreciate this is unpalatable for some, but Julie did this for years when she bought her first flat, with her flatmate's rent covering the mortgage. We've also rented out rooms in our house for the past five years, a move which

---

[48] *www.independent.co.uk/money/spend-save/spare-room-rent-lodgers-money-extra-income-household-budget-bills-a8823971.html*

brought forwards our ability to leave work several years early. When I first started post-graduate studies, I lodged with an elderly couple. Lots of people successfully rent out bedrooms without problems and with big rewards.

The UK government allows anyone to earn £7,500 a year letting out a furnished room without paying tax on the income, or even reporting it to them at all if you meet certain criteria[49]. Websites like *spareroom.co.uk* and *airbnb.co.uk* will give you an idea what your income might be, and help you find lodgers if you choose to give it a go. Where we live, a double room (including utilities) rents for about £300 to £400 a month, including bills. If you rented out a room for 6 months a year at £350 a month, and invested the income at 7% annual return, you'd be looking at a pot of around £132,000 after 25 years (even if you never increase the rent).

How willing we are to do our own jobs around the house will also make a dramatic difference to our wealth over time. Bringing in a tradesman to tile a small bathroom's walls might cost £750, when the same job could be done yourself for the materials-only cost of £200. Julie and I have tiled five bathrooms over time, saving us over £2,500. Not a huge amount alone, but extended to more and more jobs over several decades, the savings increase and increase.

A couple of other ideas for reducing housing costs (these examples assume inflation at 3% and investment return of 7% per year):

- Use cost-comparison sites to switch to cheaper utility and broadband providers. *uswitch.com* gives average annual savings of £387 for those who changed gas and electricity provider[50]. Invested over 40 years that £387 would add £113,000 to your net worth.

---

[49] *www.gov.uk/rent-room-in-your-home/the-rent-a-room-scheme*
[50] *www.uswitch.com/faqs/savings-messages*

Part Four: An Efficiently Spent Life

- A 25 square foot self-storage facility, roughly the size of a small garden shed, costs £19.19 per week for a year's let. That equates to £997.88 a year. If we could avoid using that storage and invested the money instead, over a 40-year period we'd be left with £292,000.

Where you live in the country affects the proportion of your income you'll spend on housing. Those with roots where they live, jobs, friends and family won't want to leave just to get lower housing costs, but if it is an option it can make a big difference. The fact Julie and I were brought up in the East Midlands has helped us on our own quest to get financially-free. The Housing Affordability data for England and Wales from the ONS[51] shows there is a line very roughly between The Wash and the Bristol Channel, north of which houses tend to cost less relative to wages. In other words, it's easier to become a non-trepreneur above the line than below.

Taking salary differences into account, houses are generally more expensive in the south and west of England than across the rest of England and Wales

---

[51] *www.ons.gov.uk/peoplepopulationandcommunity/housing/bulletins/housingaffordabilityinenglandandwales/2019*

Perhaps most importantly of all, there's the question of the type of neighbourhood you live in. Julie and I live in an ex coal-mining area of Nottinghamshire. Our town has a good range of amenities, is a stone's throw from countryside and has good transport links to nearby cities and the Peak District national park. It's a nice place to live while we're in the UK. It feels to us like there is zero pressure from neighbours to drive specific brands of car, to talk about which golf club we're a member of or which Caribbean island we're holidaying in this year. If anything, the pressure is the other way around: to not show conspicuous wealth. This has had a huge effect on our ability to transform our income into investments.

Big Cost Two: Transport

Cars and commuting in general are expensive. Far more expensive than we perhaps imagine, both in terms of hard cash, and in terms of our life energy, our ability to do more useful and fulfilling things with our time. Many of us think in terms of fuel alone when mentally assessing the cost of a car, missing the fact depreciation can easily equal the cost of fuel[52], never mind the lost opportunity cost of having all that money sunk into a car (you could have invested it a cash generating asset).

One analysis has shown UK car owners incur an average cost of £3,100 per car per year[53]. Take the example of a couple running two cars. Let's see what happens if they remove the need for one car (by living in walking or cycling distance to work), and they consistently invest that £3,100. At an average return of 7% over twenty years, they're missing out on £127,000. Over 40 years that missed opportunity compounds up to £610,000, even assuming the cost of driving doesn't increase. How many of us take this into account when we choose where to live and work?

---

[52] *www.theaa.com/car-buying/depreciation*
[53] *www.nimblefins.co.uk/average-cost-run-car-uk*

Throughout our careers we both commuted, mostly by car. My first commute was around 50 miles a day, and would often see me sat stationary, despondent in traffic in the dark early morning hours of winter, or the sunny evenings in autumn. I never considered the cost of it, it was more the mental aspect which I struggled with, the sense of many wasted hours, which eventually pushed me to look for work closer to home.

I also learned to ride a motorbike to enable me to get through traffic jams on the way into cities. In retrospect I could have cycled or even run the shorter commutes, but I was too out-of-shape and demotivated. Perhaps the biggest accidental financial advantage I had was the fact I was never into expensive cars or motorbikes. I was happy to drive vehicles which were ten or even twenty years old (and still am), avoiding the huge depreciation costs many colleagues were quietly hit with. I once joked with one co-worker that my car was worth roughly what he paid each month to lease his. He replied that he needed a reliable vehicle, a fair retort, although with yearly servicing I find older cars tend to be reliable these days (plus I could have easily afforded a spare car or two just sat around for the amount he was spending).

Big Cost Three: Recreation & Culture

Package holidays, TV licences and subscriptions, sports clubs and gyms, theatres, gambling, pet food and vet costs, garden plants and equipment, games and toys, computers and photography equipment, and more fill this category. According to the ONS[54], the average UK household spends £4,139 a year on all these areas combined.

---

[54] *www.ons.gov.uk/peoplepopulationandcommunity/personalandhouseholdfinances/expenditure/bulletins/familyspendingintheuk/april2018tomarch2019*

The Non-Trepreneurs

There are opportunities galore for savings here. Arguably, everything in this area is effectively a luxury, a want rather than a need so it could be cut out completely (harsh, but true). While we were working, we felt the opposite, that each of the small 'rewards' we bought for ourselves were essential for life, for our mental health. I see this all around me: the luxury purchases we make to give ourselves a pick-me-up before ploughing on with the day-to-day grind which in turn leaves us feeling down again. Julie and I inadvertently escaped this cycle when we took what we thought was a career break in our late 30s. As we started to move towards relieving ourselves of the burden of the rat race, we felt we needed far fewer of these 'essential luxuries'.

Let's take TV again, using our own situation as an example. We used to pay around £40 a month for TV subscriptions. We could easily afford it and didn't think much about it until we started to look at how it could help pay our mortgage off. We reduced our package to £25 a month, saving £180 a year, when we realised we were paying for channels we never watched. Later we shifted to Freeview TV, saving a further £300 a year (£480 in total). Let's have a look at what that money could have been worth if we'd invested it. We've assumed a 7% return and that the cost of the TV package would have increased by 3% each year with inflation:

Year	Amount Saved per Year	Investment Return @ 7%	Total Invested Wealth
1	£480	£0	£480
2	£494	£34.60	£1,008
3	£509	£35.65	£1,588
4	£525	£36.72	£2,223
5	£540	£37.82	£2,919
...	...		...
20	£842	£58.92	£24,763
30	£1,131	£79.18	£62,220
40	£1,520	£106.41	£140,549

If we'd invested the TV package money, we'd have almost £25,000 after two decades, or over £140,000 after a full 40 year working life. We'll use these same '3% inflation, 7% investment return' figures for the rest of our examples.

Gym membership is often quoted in articles about thrifty living. We use a local municipal gym from time-to-time, although we tend to spend most of our time running outside to get our exercise. Our gym costs about £30 a month, so for both of us £720 a year. If we invest that money instead, our wealth would increase by over £10,000 a decade.

This method of cumulative, long-term thinking makes us consider each purchase more intently. It doesn't prevent us from making all these purchases, we just make them less often and with far more thought. We appreciate and value them much more too.

Big Cost Four: Food

On average UK households spend £3,200 a year on groceries, and a further £1,500 on eating takeaways and at restaurants and cafes (and another £480 a year on alcoholic drinks out)[55]. We have to eat, so how are cost savings possible?

The obvious one is shifting away from any habitual eating out, including take-aways. By paying someone else to stand over the stove and sink, we're gradually impoverishing ourselves, it's that simple. If we can avoid that £25 Friday night takeaway, we might easily save ourselves £1000 a year. That amount invested would grow to £15,500 over a decade, or over £50,000 after 20 years.

While working Julie and I started taking our own food to eat at breakfast and lunchtime in the office. I recall also attracting the ire

---

[55] *www.ons.gov.uk/peoplepopulationandcommunity/ personalandhouseholdfinances/expenditure/bulletins/familyspendingintheuk/april2018tomarch2019*

of workmates for drinking the free coffee available to us, rather than the £1.50-a-go decent stuff from the canteen downstairs. Fair enough, that machine coffee was pretty bad! All the same, these habits saved around £10 a day per person. For both of us that equates to £4,400 a year, invested that could equate to over £68,000 in a decade.

Our shopping habits also changed outside of work. We both eat meat, cheese, fresh salad, nuts and fish, all relatively expensive elements of anyone's groceries bills. While we've probably reduced our red meat intake, the main shift we made was towards eating more unbranded produce choosing the supermarket's own brand or their budget brand (often found on the bottom shelves). We also buy short-life (yellow-sticker) reduced meat and fish and freeze it. Also, we do some of our core-item shopping at lower cost/budget supermarkets such as Lidl.

Big Cost Five: Children

We don't have children, so can only draw second-hand conclusions in this area. Reports vary wildly, as do people's lifestyles, but suggest that the cost to bring up a child in the UK from birth to the age of 18 ranges from £75,000 to £200,000.

Julie and I didn't choose not to have children to avoid the cost. We made the decision well before we opted to leave our well-paid jobs, and the thought of saving money by remaining childless never crossed our minds. Don't let this put you off if you have, or plan to have children though. There are plenty of blogs out there written by early retirees with children, for example:

- Barney Whiter at *theescapeartist.me* left his job aged 43. He and his wife have three children.
- Joe Udo at *retireby40.org* left work aged 36 to become a stay-at-home-dad to his child.

Part Four: An Efficiently Spent Life

- Liz and Nate at *frugalwoods.com* are financially independent but have opted not to retire; they have two young daughters.
- Winnie and Jeremy at *gocurrycracker.com* quit work in their 30s and have since had a son.
- Pete Adeney at *mrmoneymustache.com* retired aged 30 along with his wife and had a son afterwards.
- Justin at *rootofgood.com* retired aged 33 with three kids.
- Jim at *routetoretire.com* left his corporate job aged 43 with his wife Lisa and a young daughter.
- David Cox at *iretiredyoung.net* stopped working aged 47 along with his wife. They have two grown-up children.

Some non-trepreneur couples deliberately plan to start a family after they're financially-free. They work hard for a decade or two, with both of their salaries enabling a very high savings rate without the cost of childcare. This allows them to get their investments in place and then start a family, by this point one or both parents can stay at home if they wish, since the need to work has been removed.

A Thousand Cuts from the Smaller Knives

Big costs-aside, we constantly make smaller spending decisions which decide our long-term financial health. Hammering the point home once again: the oft-ridiculed example is buying take-out coffee. A one-a-weekday Starbucks or Costa habit will cost maybe £2.50 a day, not a fat lot, £625 a year. Compounded up 7% investment returns, again with 3% inflation, that coffee habit has knocked £10,000 from your wealth after a decade. Of course, not everything can be reduced to purely a financial decision, some of us like good coffee and it gives us a boost before a hard day's work. It's a balance, and one where we frequently only consider the pleasant effects of consumption, not the long-term impact on our financial health.

The same example can be applied to a huge range of smaller habits: an after-work pint in the pub, nail manicures, ordering books from

Amazon, having an all-you-can-eat package on your phone, buying lottery tickets and scratch cards, smoking, magazine subscriptions, accepting renewal quotes from insurers and energy companies without shopping around, they go on and on.

I'm terrible at doing maths in my head. Advertisers and marketeers know this and take advantage of it to get me to spend. Under a hire purchase agreement, a £25,000 car becomes far more palatable when advertised at £471.14 a month[56]. My grey matter's not up to the job of calculating the fact if I buy it this way, I'll be spending £4504.40 in interest alone over a 5-year term, the car will cost almost £30,000.

Similarly, a new top-end smartphone is advertised at £42.00 a month with a £149.00 upfront cost, a very affordable-sounding proposition. The website selling the phone has a *Show Total Cost of Ownership* button, which reveals the phone costs a minimum of £1157.00 over the length of the contract, a very different-sounding number.

Pet ownership is something else to consider delaying if you're striving for financial independence. Research by one organisation[57] placed the minimum cost of looking after a dog for its entire life at between £4,500 and £13,000, depending on the size and breed of dog. The cost of buying the dog is dwarfed by the costs of food, insurance, pet walkers, inoculations and medication. However, we did find that while our dog Charlie was alive, he helped us to save money. We didn't like to leave him alone for too long, so would choose walks in the countryside with him instead of paying to go somewhere. He also limited our eating out options, but we didn't mind, we preferred his company to any meal.

---

[56] *www.moneyadviceservice.org.uk/en/articles/buying-a-car-through-hire-purchase*
[57] *www.pdsa.org.uk/taking-care-of-your-pet/looking-after-your-pet/puppies-dogs/the-cost-of-owning-a-dog*

Part Four: An Efficiently Spent Life

Our Cost Tracking System

The Household Profit & Loss (HPL) we talked about on page 63 is useful for highlighting the small, otherwise-hidden costs which eat away at our income. Tracking these costs has evolved into an ingrained habit for us. This section looks at how we track our costs and build our HPL each month.

Julie is the cost-tracker in our house. While I enjoy the more theoretical part of personal finance, Julie has the patience to keep detailed and consistent records. She started off over a decade ago tracking our larger costs, the easier ones to find like our mortgage and utility bills. These costs were put into a spreadsheet so we could see our monthly expenses in advance and pay ourselves first. As soon as our salaries hit our bank account a chunk was moved out to pay off our mortgage.

When we started travelling, she switched to more accurate tracking, making a note of every purchase in a notebook she carries, and later transferring it to a spreadsheet which we use as our HPL. That spreadsheet is now a monster, with nine years of categorised spending, we know exactly where our money went (and where our income came from).

Many non-trepreneurs automate this tracking process using apps like *moneydashboard.com*, *www.moneyhub.com* and *yolt.com*, but we've been happier tracking our costs manually. When I say 'we', I openly admit I don't have what it takes to do that level of tracking and I'm lucky to have someone do it for me!

Dragged Down by Deprivation?

I didn't opt for the non-trepreneur approach (or even become aware of it) until my late 30s. Before that I spent. I was never into cars, but I bought a string of motorbikes, at least one with a loan. I had the original Apple iPad as soon as it appeared on the shelves and grabbed the first smartphones immediately, swapping them every

The Non-Trepreneurs

year or two. I had a garage full of tools, gym equipment and push bikes. I spent an ungodly amount of money on computer textbooks, many of which remained unread.

Despite only needing one bedroom, Julie and I started life together in a two-bed bungalow before moving into a three-bed detached house. We bought a hot tub and spent £800 a year on electricity and chemicals to run it. A campervan arrived from a nearby dealer which depreciated by around £5,000 before we sold it a few years later, halving in value. We spent two weeks in the Maldives on honeymoon, leaving with a bill longer than War & Peace.

We don't regret any of that part of our lives, and it was perhaps critical to what came next. We don't feel like we've missed out. When I'm in a hardware shop, for example, I look around and realise I've already bought practically every tool in there, at one point or another. However, if Julie and I (mainly I, she was never a big spender) were aware of, and bought into, the non-trepreneur life in our 20s, we'd have been able to quit in our mid-30s.

A common criticism of the non-trepreneur approach to gaining financial freedom is the deprived life the proponents are deemed to be inflicting upon themselves. The shift we made in our late 30s and early 40s could easily be viewed as overly frugal. Julie and I have spent most of our time in the last decade living in small spaces, as small as 6m by 2m for over four years in a motorhome. We now live on roughly £20,000 a year, having previously been earning a combined salary of around £100,000. We eat out maybe once a month and eat take-aways a couple of times a month, depending on where we are.

Do we feel deprived? No, not in the least. Why not? I'm not sure? Reading that paragraph back it sounds like we should feel we're denying ourselves too much in return for not needing to work. But it doesn't really feel that way. My feeling is we know what it feels like to be able to buy what we wanted, when we wanted it, so we don't have the frustration associated with self-denial. We know we could buy pretty much anything we wanted, but it wasn't making us happy, it was having the opposite effect.

It's important to make the point that we're a million miles from anything approaching poverty. We spend relatively little, but we have a huge safety net protecting us from ever being cold, hungry, not having a roof over our heads or suffering the crushing lack of hope poverty entails.

We can buy whatever we want to, although we spend time thinking about and researching non-essential purchases. We recently replaced both our smartphones, having previously self-replaced components in them both to extend their lives. We train in £100 running shoes, although we tend to buy last season's models to bring the costs down to around £60 a pair. We both have GPS running watches. Mine costs £480 new, although I went for an officially refurbished watch which was £170 cheaper, and Ju's was second-hand from eBay. We can spend months at a time travelling across Europe in our motorhome, mostly staying on campsites or official parking. We have all we need, and our budget allows us to replace gadgets, clothes and so on as needed.

What's more, frugality can be fun. We enjoy being different. It's entertaining to find bargains at local charity shops (including branded gear with the original labels attached) and to outwit the supermarkets by comparing the cost per kg rather than rely on what they are promoting. We even enjoy trying to read the small print on TV ads to see how much interest they are charging or how much the item they are showing you costs compared to the price on the screen. We recently met a roofer who was happy for us to remove a load of old roof slats from his skip. We carried them home in several trips, removed all the nails and sawed them up. Instead of landfill they'll start our wood-burner for half a winter, which gives us a warm glow in two ways, cracking!

We've both done more than our fair share of consuming the world's resources, so we have no soap box to stand on and declare we should all be buying less stuff. There are, of course, plenty of arguments for consuming less in order to reduce our human impact on the environment. However, for Julie and me, it's a happy co-incidence that the frugality which drives our freedom leads naturally to a smaller footprint on the planet.

The More Radical Options
If you're in the mood for a more radical change in your life, then here are options some non-trepreneurs pursue which can speed up the path to financial independence.

Geoarbitrage
Some choose to use something called 'geographic arbitrage' sometimes shortened to 'geoarbitrage' to speed up their journey to financial independence. This is a simple concept: they deliberately look for places to live where their income goes further.

Geoarbitrage can be applied both to moving within your home country and moving abroad. Here in the UK, using job search websites can give you an idea how well your role pays in different areas of the country. You can then compare this with house prices, pulling information from websites like *zoopla.com*. I worked in IT, with jobs placed on *jobserve.com*, and I'd often find that London jobs paid similar amounts to jobs in the Midlands, while the cost of living in the South East is much higher.

Heading abroad, sites like *numbeo.com* give quick overviews of where the lower cost of living countries are. In a sense we're lucky in the UK as our cost of living is relatively high, matched by relatively high earning capabilities. This means we can potentially take our Sterling passive income from rental property, share funds and so on and get far more for it abroad.

Part Four: An Efficiently Spent Life

Another site that is fun to play with is *www.theearthawaits.com* which allows you to indicate your monthly budget, family size, whether you want to live in a city centre and so on. For us Brits, the obvious countries which spring to mind are Spain, Portugal and France. These are all relatively close to the UK for visits home, have better climates than the British Isles and have a lower cost of living. There are options across the planet though, depending on your sense of adventure.

A quick comparison on *numbeo.com* shows that it's 20% cheaper to live in Málaga in southern Spain than here in Nottingham. If you spend £2,500 a month in Nottingham, you'd only need £2,000 a month in Málaga. Using a safe withdrawal rate of 4% (we'll come onto this later), your investment target reduces from £750,000 to £600,000 as a result. These are all 'average' numbers of course and don't consider personal circumstances like any need to make frequent journeys to the UK.

Julie and I have travelled widely across Europe and North Africa, but we've opted to keep the UK as our base country, at least for now. This removes issues we'd need to consider if we chose to move abroad permanently: visas or residency requirements, language, taxation, health care, security and political stability, visiting family and friends and so on. Our costs are higher while we're in the UK, but we can easily spend a few months at a time in lower cost countries, and we don't spend a huge amount anyway so we're not penalising ourselves a great deal.

Browsing the financial independence blogs out there, I don't come across many stories of people going for the option of moving abroad. I have found a couple of examples, like Jim from *routetoretire.com*, an American who moved with his wife and daughter to Panama with the expectation their expenses would be reduced. Jeremy and Winnie of *gocurrycracker.com* retired in their 30s and have since spent their time travelling and living mostly in

101

low-cost of living countries. In general, most non-trepreneurs seem to want to stay where they already live.

Extreme Downsizing

Another option to get your target figure down, speeding up your departure point from the mandatory job, is to drastically cut your housing expenses with extreme downsizing. By this I mean typically shifting from a bricks-n-mortar house to either a room in a shared house or into a motorhome, caravan or a boat.

Julie and I have used this approach to cut several years from our working lives, selling or giving away many of our possessions and living in a combination of a shared house and a motorhome. For the past six years we've lived as a couple in spaces less than 30m², about a third of the size of the average UK home.

In our shared home in the UK our bills are shared with tenants, plus there's always someone here when we're away travelling, avoiding issues with home insurance and keeping the house safe. There are downsides of course, but the compromises for us have been worth the reward. When we're not in the UK we travel freely in a motorhome, a space of around 10m². We found we could travel 'full-time' (living in a motorhome all year round) and tour from the Arctic to the Sahara for around £20,000 a year. This covers all costs, including the depreciation on our vehicle, meaning this amount, increasing with inflation, would be sustainable for us long-term.

As I mentioned earlier, we considered the option of moving onto a narrowboat at one point, moored in a marina on a canal near where we were renting a house. We could buy a used narrowboat for £30,000 to £40,000 (*narrowboats.apolloduck.co.uk* is fun to browse). We'd then need to pay for a license for the boat, plus marina fees, insurance, buy a safety certificate and budget for maintenance such as periodically 'blacking' the bottom of the boat and looking after the engine.

We pulled together all the boat costs and compared them with the option of buying a house. For us, this showed that yes, our day-to-day costs would be lower compared with a house, but over the long term boats tend to depreciate while houses tend to appreciate, and our guesstimate spreadsheet showed that after a decade our wealth would be roughly £50,000 higher if we bought a house. In the end we opted to buy a house for this reason, although we've an open mind to the idea of moving onto a boat in the future.

Moving into a relatively small space can never be just a question of cost though, it is a lifestyle compromise. Working at home can be awkward, it's a little difficult to hold a house party in such a small space and we've little room to store possessions, but that helps stop us buying more stuff! Julie and I have found, for whatever reason, that the compromises involved happen to suit us.

In Summary
We tend to go through life making the same lifestyle spending decisions as our family, friends, co-workers and neighbours. By taking these societal spending cues we find ourselves spending most, if not all our income, regardless of how much we earn. This removes the possibility of us building wealth outside of our pensions, making work a necessity until we're in our 50s or more likely our 60s.

Few of us are born with the ability to multiply up relatively small costs over months or years, and even fewer (definitely not me) can mentally assess the compound effect we'd experience if we invested the money we saved. How often do we pull out a spreadsheet to assess whether to take a boxed lunch to work, or even whether to take on significant debt with a mortgage or car loan?

The Non-Trepreneurs

By being more mindful and aware of the freedom-stealing effect of our spending habits, we can decide where the benefits of spending don't outweigh the long-term drain on our energy and liberty. By altering our habits to spend more efficiently, we also make it easier to have a long, fun and fulfilling multi-decade post-work period by reducing our investment target.

Part Five: Increasing Income

"Things flow to you, when you do your part first."

Tony Robbins, American Author and Philanthropist

To use the non-trepreneur approach to get free of mandatory work, we needed to:

- earn as much as we could,
- reduce our spending,
- and see wealth as freedom, not spending power.

We've already looked at changing your mindset and finding out where your money goes, on both the obvious and not-so-obvious costs. Let's now have a look at ways in which Julie and I increased our incomes over our two decades of paid work.

Continual Education

I have a degree in Physics while Julie did a BTEC in Photography, having failed her A levels (she was busy learning to play pool). We both took very different paths into the world of work, but we both ended up on above-average incomes.

You don't need a degree to aim for the non-trepreneur life, but it helps. Graduates earn a median salary of £34,000 in the UK, and non-graduates £25,000[58]. Even accounting for student loan debt, graduates will (on average) out-earn non-graduates.

---

[58] *explore-education-statistics.service.gov.uk/find-statistics/graduate-labour-markets*

Having a degree made it relatively easy for me, I think, to get my first job as a technical writer. I remember writing an earnest covering letter saying I'd recently written a user manual for a system I was using at university, and how much I enjoyed hard work. Twenty-six years later I can still feel the nerves of being interviewed by first the team manager, and on a second occasion by one of the co-owners of the company. Having that qualification on my CV was instrumental in getting me in the door.

Julie's career began working in a shop at the weekend, taking extra shifts in the week to cover sickness or holidays. Once she finished college, she started out as a temporary secretary. After securing a permanent position, she took on more and more responsibility as each small opportunity arose.

Over the years we both continued to educate ourselves, either taking opportunities provided by work or going it alone. Julie went to night school for three years to become a chartered marketeer, I took various courses on software testing, service management, project management and network engineering. I had a library of computer books which filled a bookcase, and spent many evenings and weekend studying, often informally sat in front of the TV, but it was a never-ending process (until it did end that is, when I quit the corporate arena).

I can't quantify with any accuracy what additional income all the career education generated for us. My gut feeling is it probably roughly doubled our salaries over the years.

Doing What Others Won't

I can remember trying to work out what it took to progress up the corporate career ladder. I imagined I'd only get so far, because I was from the wrong kind of background. I was working class. I had a local accent. I didn't know anyone of importance, and I didn't have any in-built sense that I could lead people.

As it turned out, I was looking at the problem the wrong way. The way in which I progressed, whether I'd realised it or not, was simple: to do what those around me wouldn't.

The corporate world I inhabited was packed with cynicism. At least that's how I interpreted it at the time. Engineers and team leaders would shake their heads at the ineptitude of the managers around and above them. They'd decry new projects as pointless, poorly thought-through and doomed to fail. I should know, I was one of the cynics, to a degree at least. My colleagues and I would mentally point at those above us and blame them for our lack of personal progress. I can't recall a single one of us looking in the mirror and criticising ourselves. None of us said: "I'm the blocker. If I'm to move up, I need to improve". As American author and motivational speaker Jim Rohn said:

"If you want to have more, you have to become more. Success is not something you pursue. What you pursue will elude you; it can be like trying to chase butterflies. Success is something you attract by the person you become."

Whenever I shifted up the ladder, it was because I took on more responsibility. In order to do that, I had to first force myself to believe I was capable of that next step up. I had to overcome the fear of failure, of not being liked by the people I managed, of looking a fool. In other words, I had to grow as a person, and that in turn led to a growth in income.

Going Self-Employed

In information technology (IT), there's demand for short-term workers. Projects arise which usually only last for a few months but might need far more staff than the company employs on a permanent basis or they may need some specific expertise for a short period of time.

Contract (or freelance) employees fill this gap. These are usually self-employed and paid on a day rate. They're not employees, so the company doesn't need to make pension contributions or furnish them with sick pay, holiday pay, accrue for maternity/paternity leave, national insurance, company cars, training and so on. Assuming they work the usual 220 days a year or more, they can take home double what a full-time employee would be paid.

The main downside is the fact contract staff have no job security: they could be laid off within a week, in a downturn or if a project is cancelled. They also have to manage their own finances, setting up their own pension, saving for the days they don't want to or can't work, paying their own taxes and submitting formal records to the Inland Revenue.

As a team leader responsible for 15 engineers, I frequently used contract staff to bolster our numbers when upgrading systems and so on. With a mortgage to pay, no experience of going self-employed, and not enough self-belief that I could make it as a contractor, I didn't have the courage to try it.

It was only after we'd left work for two years and returned, with renewed vigour and free of our mortgage, that I dared give contract work a go. Within three weeks of looking for a contract position I walked back through the doors of my old company, this time being paid a day rate and working for myself. I was given a phone and a long list of employees and asked to phone them up and talk to them about handing in an old laptop they still had. For this my pay was doubled, bizarre but true.

After some months I moved back into project management and had to earn that high fee, being responsible for a £1m project. While I was one of the newest contract project managers, one person in my team had been running a landscape gardening company a couple of years beforehand, and another was only a year or two from university. I'd built up over 16 years' experience in various companies, projects and roles before I dared try my hand at going it alone, more fool me!

Self-employment is a risk, but for those who are willing to take the risk and do the job better than their competitors, it's a faster path to building wealth. That's assuming you can resist spending all the money on luxury cars, five-bedroom houses, Champagne-fuelled meals out, horses and Rolex watches!

I don't know whether self-employment is possible in your field, or in a field you're willing to move into. The increased earnings don't just apply to IT though, that much is certain. One set of statistics[59] reports the following differences in tradespeople working for an employer (PAYE) or for themselves.

Trade	PAYE	Self-Employed
Electrician	£27,287	£51,200
Landscape Gardener	£24,454	£40,140
Plumber	£23,877	£36,359

This is only one set of figures, and these differences could be exaggerated by a greater proportion of self-employed tradespeople being more experienced, but the variances are worth considering, nevertheless.

Value Yourself

At the start of my freelancing career I knew the management were reluctant to renegotiate daily rates once a contractor was in the door. It took a few self-administered face slaps to build up the courage, but I told the hiring manager I'd only take a role if they paid £50 per day above the rate they'd offered. The result came back

---

[59] *www.moneywise.co.uk/news/2019-05-08%E2%80%8C%E2%80%8C/electricians-named-biggest-earners-amongst-self-employed-professionals*

The Non-Trepreneurs

quickly: yeah, no problem. That single request 'earned' us an additional £20,000 over the 23 months of contracts I completed for this company.

The point I'm trying to make is this: don't undervalue yourself. If you're not being paid the market rate, ask for a raise or look for a job elsewhere within a short distance of your home which will pay you what you're worth. The money is out there, and if your skills and attitude are up to scratch, then it should flow to you.

Ready-Made Side Gigs

It's my strong belief that the skills you already have for your main day job, or can acquire through training, are those which will drive your ability to earn. However, to help speed things up, there are various 'ready-made' side gigs that you could consider to build additional income. In other words, they're ideal non-trepreneur territory. These part-time jobs can also be very useful if you opt to quit your main day job once you're financially-independent, as they will bolster your investment income, keep you engaged with the world around you and give you targets to aim for. Here are some side-gig jobs I've come across over time. We've done some of these ourselves:

- Network marketing companies like Avon, Utility Warehouse, Ann Summers and Neal's Yard.
- Selling home-made craftwork on Etsy (*www.etsy.com/uk*)
- Dog walking or pet sitting.
- Gig economy jobs like Uber driving, or Deliveroo deliveries.
- Renting out a spare room with Rent-a-Room or AirBnB.
- Using publishing platforms like Amazon's KDP to self-publish a book (*kdp.amazon.com*).
- If you've the skills: setting up websites, designing logos, teaching a musical instrument, become a DJ, selling your photos, running a nightclass or bootcamp and so on.

Earning from Investments

As soon as you start to invest in cash-flow-positive assets, they'll start to throw money at you too, albeit in a small way at first. By re-investing that income you speed up the time it takes to hit your FI target. We'll go into more detail in the next part, but it's worth remembering that as well as building your investments using money saved from your day job, your investments will also build themselves.

The higher the amount you have invested, the more help they will give you. Once you've £100,000 in an index tracking share fund, it should 'naturally' generate £6,000 to £7,000 a year in capital gains and dividends (averaged over the long-term). With you doing absolutely nothing, that's the power of passive income.

In Summary

The more income we can generate from our jobs, without succumbing to the temptations around us to spend the lot, the faster we're able to build the cash engines described in the next part of the book. The faster those engines grow, the quicker our escape from the rat race is enabled.

Remember to think in non-trepreneurial timescales, decades rather than months. Our incomes didn't just magically increase, we dedicated years to self-education, we took on leadership roles which were well outside our comfort zones, we opted to use self-employment to give us the possibility of an earnings boost. It seems likely anyone wanting to build their income will need to take similar steps, but I imagine anyone with the vision and drive to attain early financial freedom won't be lacking the energy needed.

Part Six: Building Cash Engines

"Investing should be more like watching paint dry or watching grass grow. If you want excitement, take $800 and go to Las Vegas."

Paul Samuelson, American Economist and Nobel Prize Winner

I don't know how much income my parents have never mind what savings they might have. I doubt I'm all that unusual in this. How many Brits discuss finances with their parents, friends and colleagues in any detail? None that I know of, other than the odd flash of conversation about how much someone spent on a house or car, or perhaps how much someone just made selling some shares.

Nevertheless, my early financial education largely came from my parents. They taught me to avoid debt (other than a mortgage), and to save money. They both came from backgrounds of poverty, so it's no surprise they weren't educated about investing. They couldn't pass on to me knowledge and experience they didn't have.

Despite having a degree which involved advanced maths, personal finance and investing remained an area I simply avoided thinking about for the first two decades of my adult life. Thankfully I took advice to start contributing a portion of my income into occupational pensions from the age of 22. I knew my employers were also contributing something and had some idea about there being a tax incentive, but other than that I was clueless. I didn't understand the funds the pensions were invested in, what risks were involved with those funds, what fees I was being charged or what happens with those pensions at the point I retired.

Part Six: Building Cash Engines

It was only when I'd turned 41, when we came back from our two-year career break and had thrust ourselves back into the corporate world, that I started to educate myself. I found websites and library books which, for the grand price of nothing, had a wealth of easy-to-understand information. Where necessary we bought books, which generated enormous returns for the small costs involved.

These resources revealed that the maths of investing was straightforward, percentages and probability were the hardest concepts involved. The terminology was the most difficult thing to grasp, but once I'd actively worked at understanding it, that wasn't hard. Putting what I'd learned into practice though? That was tough.

Accidental Investors

The investments which currently power our early retirement were largely accidental ones. When the housing market crashed, we found ourselves owning a bungalow, which we'd moved out of into a larger house, but could only sell at a large discount. We had mortgages on both properties, not the brightest of moves. Getting a little desperate, we decided to rent the bungalow out to cover the mortgage payments and became 'accidental' landlords. We never assessed the bungalow in terms of costs and returns, it just happened to work out for us. Some years later we let out the larger house too, when we set off travelling, and when we returned left it let, another accidental investment.

Since then we've bought a property as a deliberate investment, part of which is a small shop. We've also educated ourselves enough to feel confident investing over £100,000 in shares in our ISAs and have taken all but one of our pensions into direct control as SIPPs, self-invested personal pensions. We continue to invest as we're still saving money 'in retirement'. We're far from expert investors and, by many non-trepreneur's standards, have only modest housing and equity portfolios.

Our Non-Trepreneur Investing Principles

These principles underpin the way in which we currently invest. They come from a mixture of experience and from reading a wide variety of books and blogs, drawing on the advice of seasoned investing professionals.

The principles apply to our specific scenario: we need to fund a retirement for two people for maybe 40 years. We should also reiterate that we've only deliberately been investing for the past six years. Before that we were accidental landlords, and we don't consider ourselves in any way expert investors. We've put these into this book only to get you thinking about what type of investor you want to be.

Principle 1: Emergency Fund First

The value of our houses and shares ride up and down with market conditions. This is completely natural and to-be-expected. However, we don't want to find ourselves in a position where we're in need of cash at a point when the markets are down, forcing us to sell an investment at a loss. For this reason, we hold an emergency fund in cash (in sterling, as most of our spending is done in the UK) and cash-like assets (Premium Bonds in our case). These cover at least two year's living expenses.

The downside of keeping so much money in cash is the fact it will lose value over time, as interest rates are less than inflation. We accept this in return for the ability to sleep easy at night, knowing we have such a large and soft mattress to break our fall in case something goes badly wrong.

Principle 2: No Mortgage Debt on Our Main Home

We paid the mortgage off on our main home before we understood the basics of investing. As a result, it never occurred to us we might get a greater return on our money if we invested it rather than clearing the mortgage debt. With mortgage interest rates down at

3%, say, and long-term index fund returns of 7%, it would have made more financial sense to have an interest-only mortgage and plough the money into our stocks and shares ISAs instead.

However, with the benefit of hindsight, I think we'd still have paid the mortgage off on our main home. The effect of being mortgage-free was a hugely freeing one for us, we felt lighter and happier without it (and still do). We felt more carefree when it came to taking risks, like leaving work to travel. For us, the emotional benefits trumped the strictly financial ones in this case.

Principle 3: We Need Income

We need to pay our bills and pay for fun stuff, which requires cash. We could buy gold bullion (surprisingly easy to do), hope it goes up in value and then sell it, but we're not convinced we can forecast the price of precious metals. Same goes for buying houses and 'flipping them', tidying them up and selling them again in the hope we can get a better price. I have no doubt there are folks making a good profit buying and selling gold and houses in this way, but I'm also sure there is a quieter number of people breaking even or making a loss.

Our circumstances mean that we need investments which will generate an income for several decades. We've opted to rent out houses and a small shop, which creates a steady monthly income. Two of our property's roofs have solar panels installed and we receive monthly payments for the electricity they generate. Over the past six years, we've slowly built up our share investments, which pay out dividends every three months. As mentioned above, our emergency fund is held in Premium Bonds which usually 'win' an interest payment each month. All these smaller income streams add up to cover our expenses.

Principle 4: We're Low-to-Medium Risk Takers

We've investments in government bonds (low risk), solar panels (low risk), houses (medium risk), our small shop (medium risk) and index-tracking share funds (medium risk). All these assessments of risk are our own, the way we personally feel about the investments. We're also willing to hold onto each investment for decades, reducing risk of loss from short-term market crashes. To keep our risk to a minimum we avoid:

- **Investing in individual shares.** We've done this more than once and have tended to lose money. Other non-trepreneurs research and invest in a portfolio of high-quality companies, but it's not something we're comfortable doing.
- **Trading or flipping.** We don't try to buy shares, houses or commodities like oil or gold, with the idea we'll be able to sell them again within a few months at a profit.
- **Investing in derivatives.** We don't try to hedge our share positions with options or other derivatives, as we don't believe we can do it successfully. We're comfortable with average returns and with market volatility.

Principle 5: We Must Understand It

In February and March 2020, the value of our shares fell by almost 30% as the COVID-19 pandemic struck the world. Later, in the first half of 2022, our shares lost around 20% of their value. On both occasions the Google Sheet we use to track their value flipped from all-green to lots-of-red, denoting a loss. Although our earlier investments in shares were still worth more than we bought them for, almost all the later share investments were now showing a loss. The news was of catastrophe. Everything screamed sell, sell, SELL!!!

During that first crash in 2020 this had never happened to us before, but we didn't sell. We took the opportunity to buy a few more shares, careful to keep our emergency fund intact though. We knew from reading books written by people who've been through market crashes before, that selling is a bad idea. Why? Because the chances are, by the time we've bought our shares back, the markets are likely to have increased past the point we sold them. It sounds bizarre, but studies find this is exactly how many individual investors behave. We held onto our shares, buying a few more as the market dropped, in the knowledge they'd probably be back up again within a few years. In practice they bounced back in a period of months.

It's only because we understood the nature of the investment, and because our investments are spread across many companies, geographies and sectors rather than in individual companies, that we felt we could take this wealth-protecting action (or lack of action). Only by understanding how an investment works can we understand the risks we're exposing ourselves to and how we should behave around it. We've learned these lessons from books and blogs on investing and other aspects of personal finance and self-growth.

Principle 6: We're in it for the Long Term

Our overall goal is to produce enough income from our investments to enable us to avoid mandatory work for the remainder of our lives. We're not saving up for a house, car or holiday. Instead, we aim to own investments for decades, which will generate a long-term, year-on-year return for us. We're happy with average returns, we don't need to take the risk of trying to outperform other investors. The overall return of our portfolio only needs to exceed inflation by a few percent, enough to allow us to continue with our current standard of living.

Principle 7: We're a Low-Leverage Lot

One approach to building wealth more quickly is to use other people's money (OPM) when investing. We tend do this in the UK without even thinking about it, borrowing large amounts of OPM from banks and building societies to buy our houses. This is known as leveraging.

If a young couple buys a £150,000 house with a £15,000 deposit of their own money and a £135,000 mortgage (OPM), looking at this purchase with our non-trepreneur hats on, the couple has just made a leveraged bet on the housing market. It's unlikely (but entirely possible) that some kind of financial crisis occurs soon afterwards, which causes them to lose their jobs at the same time the housing market falls.

If the market reduces the value of their home by 10%, and they can't keep up their mortgage payments, they could lose the £15,000 they have invested. Worse still, if it drops 20%, as it did in 2008 and 2009, their house value would fall to £120,000. In this dreaded position of 'negative equity', they'd lose not just their £15,000, but another £15,000 too, if they were forced to sell. Alternatively, it could lead to their home being repossessed by the mortgage company, which happened to roughly 46,000 mortgages in 2009.

However, if the market gradually rises 10%, this same couple's home is now worth £165,000. That's a £15,000 gain on an investment of £15,000 (their deposit), a 100% increase in their equity. That's the effect of leveraging: it amplifies both losses and gains.

Here in the UK home ownership has a special place in the nation's hearts. We don't consider it a gamble. If a young couple tells the world they've just put a deposit down on their first home, we all congratulate them and don't give it a moment's thought. Imagine if that a couple told us they'd decided to borrow £135,000 of OPM to buy shares in the stock market: most people would be gob-smacked at their recklessness.

We only have a small mortgage on the bungalow we own, which is interest-only but we pay 10% off the capital amount each year to gradually reduce it to nothing. This doesn't make sense from a financial perspective, as we can earn more on investments than we pay in mortgage interest, but it's an emotional driver for us.

Part Six: Building Cash Engines

By avoiding leveraging, we won't have the opportunity to make big gains when the housing market increases, but we won't make big losses if it falls. This suits us, and the way we feel about risk.

Principle 8: We Can't Time the Market

As individual investors we don't have the expertise to know when the FTSE 100 or S&P 500 (the Standard & Poor's 500, the stock market index which tracks the value of the biggest 500 companies in the US) is high. We have no idea when it's the best time to buy or sell a house or when the value of a fund is lower than it should be.

If we could, we'd 'time the market', buying shares when they were relatively cheap and selling them when they were relatively high, ideally just before a big market crash. With the cash we'd wait until the market hit rock bottom again and then buy back far more shares than we had before, repeating the cycle until we were deca-billionaires! I've shown the perfect market timing situation below using the S&P 500 index as an example, over the past few years.

Perfect (impossible) market timing using the S&P 500 index

It's easy to recall a story of when a friend or colleague has bought a house, car, share, fund, watch or whatever and subsequently sold it for a big profit. Although this might be completely down to luck, the receiver of the windfall is (perhaps) likely to believe otherwise and tell the world loudly and proudly of their shrewdness! That same person might not to be so verbose when they make a loss on an investment, an event which might be far more frequent than their big gains, a bit like gamblers only ever telling of their wins, we'll never know.

While we might get lucky too and get one of these market timing sell-buy-sell cycles right, it's more likely we'll get the next one wrong. I don't feel too bad about this: professional investors don't stand much chance of getting it right either. So, we're happy to buy shares when we've saved up enough, or when the market crashes, and keep hold of them.

Principle 9: We Want Diversification

We could sell two of our properties (the ones we don't live in) and transfer all the money into the stock market. That would simplify our lives, potentially reduce our income tax, removing the need to worry about tenants damaging the properties, not paying rent, us needing to repair and replace built-in appliances, the roofs, windows, gas boilers and so on.

We've chosen not to do this to date as we like to own different types of asset: houses, the shop, shares, bonds and even solar panels. We've also invested in share funds rather than individual shares, so our money is split across thousands of companies of various sizes, operating in different market segments around the world.

The Investments We Use

The following section takes a look at the investments we own, why we have them, and what we see as good and bad about them.

Cash Savings

We keep roughly 6 months' worth of living expenses as cash, in a joint current account, savings accounts and cash ISAs. As I write, the official Bank of England interest rate is 1.25% and it's not been above 2% for over a decade. This means our cash is losing value in real terms as the prices of the goods and services we use inflates. If we'd placed £10,000 in an account paying the Bank of England interest rate in 2010, inflation would have eroded roughly £1,500 from its real value today, 10 years later. For this reason, although we've listed cash under this investing section, we don't currently think of it as a cash machine. If interest rates exceed inflation in future, then that assessment would change.

We hold onto cash to pay our bills, buy food, fuel, pay for insurance, clothes and day-to-day expenses, things we can't do with bonds or shares. While cash currently earns negative interest (in real terms), it does have the advantage of being protected under the Financial Services Compensation Scheme (FSCS, *www.fscs.org.uk*). This protects personal cash up to £85,000 per financial institution per person, which easily exceeds the amount of cash we hold.

Government Bonds

We have around two years' worth of living expenses held in UK Government Bonds, specifically as NS&I Premium Bonds (*www.nsandi.com/premium-bonds*). These are effectively loans made to the UK government and as such there's relatively little risk we won't be able to exchange them back into cash (in other words there's a low default risk). Individuals can currently own up to £50,000 in Premium Bonds.

Typically, bonds pay out interest like a 'normal loan', but Premium Bonds don't work like this. Instead, each bond is entered into a monthly prize draw, with a chance to win up to £1m. At present, bond holders receive an average return of around 1.4%, but as a small number of bonds win very large amounts, the real return for most bond holders is closer to 1%[60]. Again, 1% is less than inflation, so the bonds (on average) lose money over time. We own them because:

---

[60] *www.moneysavingexpert.com/savings/premium-bonds*

- We can quickly change them back to cash if we need it.
- Inflation aside, they don't go up or down in value.
- We don't gamble on the horses or the National Lottery, but we do like the small buzz we get from the monthly prize draw!

Rental Housing

We own a two-bed bungalow and a house, the latter of which we live in and share with tenants, both in the same area west of Nottingham. Both are managed through a local letting agent, who takes care of the legal paperwork for us, sourcing and checking tenants, taking and storing their deposits, receiving rent payments, arranging for gas and electrical safety checks, instructing tradesmen to make repairs, checking the properties are well-maintained and not being damaged and so on. We pay 9% plus VAT of the rent for this service, because it enables us to travel for months at a time outside the country while ensuring the tenants are looked after.

We own house we live in outright and have a relatively small interest-only buy-to-let mortgage on the bungalow. After taking away all costs, management, maintenance, void periods (when a house is empty), repairs and tax, we see a rental return of between 3% and 4% the value of equity. In other words, for each £10,000 we have invested in housing we receive £300 to £400 a year to live on. The properties are also likely appreciating in value, by maybe 2% a year (although likely much higher in 2021 and 2022), bringing our total return up to around 5% to 6% a year.

Until recently we also owned a three-bedroom detached house which we also used to live in. We opted to sell it and invest the money in shares instead, for these reasons:

- We'd been investing in share funds for eight years and were comfortable with their inherent volatility.
- The tenants weren't taking care of the house and garden, and weren't reliably paying the rent.

- The rental income was taxable, but if we could shift the investment into ISAs (which would take a few years) we could reduce our future tax bill.
- Rental income isn't as 'passive' as share income. Repairs, upgrades and worries over rent payments and tenants' dog wrecking the house all occupied our minds.

Also, the housing market was high and fast-moving at the point of sale. The house sold above the asking price to the first couple to look at it. The stock market was (and still is) at a low point too, having dropped around 20% during the first half of 2022, so the shares were 'on sale'. This was pure luck though (maybe, the stock market may fall much further, and the housing market rise much more). The timing didn't affect our decision to sell.

Only the property we currently live in was bought with an idea we might rent out the bedrooms. The other two were accidental investments. Could we have gotten a higher return if we'd deliberately chosen properties as investments? Probably. Although housing where we live is relatively cheap compared to much of the UK, there are lots of places which are cheaper while still retaining good access to schools and employment. We looked at HMOs, houses of multiple occupancy like student lets, but opted not to do this as we wanted less management overhead (not having to deal with multiple tenants, potentially yearly changes to tenants and so on).

One area we heard a lot about when reading books about property investing was the idea it's possible to get houses Below Market Value (BMV). They suggested you find homeowners having trouble paying their mortgage, buy the house from them at a discount and rent it back to them. This didn't feel right to us, so we avoided it. We later spoke with a landlord who'd done just this, subsequently having to evict the tenant who didn't pay their rent for several months, an unpleasant and expensive process (although one we've also had to go through unrelated to the BMV strategy).

There were also plenty of stories on the internet of developers finding properties which needed renovation and buying them very cheaply. We found the competition for these properties is high, everyone wants to do the same thing. We decided that average returns were good enough for us, because there was a big risk we'd spend so long trying to get somewhere cheaply we'd never actually invest (a situation known as *inertia risk*).

Property investing definitely has its downsides. Tax is a big one as we've touched on above: the UK government offers few tax breaks for buy-to-let landlords. Rent counts towards your income tax. If a rental house increases in value, it's liable for capital gains tax (CGT) when you sell it (we've just paid £9,000 in CGT). Mortgage interest can only be fully discounted from your tax bill by basic rate taxpayers. Houses are illiquid too. They take time to buy or sell and have high transaction costs for estate agents and solicitors. Ours took over a year from the decision to sell to receiving the money and cost around £4,000 in fees (plus another £3,000 in repairs).

Compare this with share funds inside a Stocks and Shares ISA. These can be bought and sold in seconds (when the exchange is open), so are highly liquid. Each trade costs roughly £10. You don't pay income tax on dividends, or capital gains tax on profits when you sell them. They don't need the gas boiler servicing and they never phone up to say the roof is leaking or they've locked themselves out. While we're comfortable with the diversification we got from property, we're under no illusions the real reason we owned the houses was the fact we didn't previously understand anything about share funds and felt safer with bricks and mortar.

Solar Panels

Our bungalow and current house have solar photo-voltaic (PV) panels on the roofs. These are attached to inverters, which convert the power they generate into the same form used by the National Grid. The power is first made available to any appliances running in the house, and any excess power is exported to the grid for others to use.

This works as an investment in two ways. Julie and I benefit from payments from a government-backed Feed-In-Tariff (FIT) scheme. A meter attached to each solar PV system indicates how much power it generates. We're paid a small amount for each unit of electricity generated. We're also paid for 50% of these units, on the assumption we used the other 50% in the home. The rates we're paid were fixed when we installed the panels. They rise with inflation though and are guaranteed for 20 years from installation. If we and our tenants use our appliances when the panels are generating energy, we will also benefit from lower electricity bills.

Combined, the two installations cost us around £10,000, and we receive roughly £1,000 a year in FIT payments. On the face of it that's a 10% return but the picture is complicated by depreciation, the system's age and risk of breaking down, so there could be additional costs in future, despite components being guaranteed.

We decided to invest in the panels to further diversify our income streams and, to be honest, as we found the systems interesting and a bit of fun. We track the income we get from the panels, but currently it's too early to tell if they are a good investment or if we would have been better off just placing the money into a passive index-tracking share fund.

Commercial Property

The last property we bought was a three-bedroom semi-detached Victorian house with an ex-butcher's shop embedded in the front. The small shop has no access to the house behind and above it. Because the house is in a conservation area on a cobbled street in the centre of our town, we decided not to try and convert the shop into part of the house and instead renovated it and let it out.

We initially let the shop out to a tenant who had no experience running a shop, and after six months they handed their notice in. Initially we managed the rental of the shop ourselves using a lease off the internet. During those six months we had to address a quite few issues with the tenants, things like plugging in cheap appliances which didn't comply with EU regulations and blew the shop electrics. When they left, we'd learned a lesson and instructed a local letting agent who deals with commercial property to source, check and manage tenants for us. For this we pay them around 6% of the rent each month.

Under the commercial agent a baker took on the shop, selling delicious artisanal food they cooked at home. They lasted less than a year before having to close down for personal reasons. The current tenants have carried out mobile phone repairs for over five years.

In commercial lease agreements the tenants are responsible for fitting out the shop to meet their needs: installing flooring, counters, shelves and so on. They're also responsible for the window glass if it's broken. In our (limited) experience, shops cause far fewer headaches with tenants, but are also more likely to be empty. Ours has rented well but has still been empty for a total of one year during the seven years we've owned it. If we had to guess the proportion of the house cost spent on the shop, we'd say we see an average annual return on investment of around 8% after management costs. The biggest risk we feel we have with the shop is it being empty for long periods of time. There are several shops nearby which have not had tenants for several years.

Stocks and Shares

Once you start browsing through FIRE blogs, equities, stocks and shares (all names for the same thing) are a very common way used by the authors to power financial independence. Julie and I recognised this around six years ago and, after doing what felt like the right amount of research, started to gradually invest in shares inside our Stocks and Shares ISAs. This is another of the advantages of share investing compared with rental housing: you can start small (just a few hundred pounds if you like) and gradually add to your investments as your confidence grows.

Shares are part ownership of a company. Anyone with a share trading account can buy shares in thousands of companies across the world, becoming part-owner in Amazon and Apple, for example, rather than being just a consumer of their products. The reason for buying shares is, hopefully, to be rewarded by the success of the company you part own. If the share value increases, you can sell them at a profit. If the company makes a profit, they can also choose to give some of this to their shareholders, referred to as dividend payments.

Many people, me included until a few years ago, saw shares as a gamble and shied away from them. While we were travelling, we met a lovely couple in their 60s who relayed how they'd invested heavily in technology shares in the late 1990s. Their investments did so well they persuaded family members to invest too. The dot com bubble burst in 2000, resulting in the technology company shares crashing and creating a huge loss for them and their family. They lost all their life savings, and taught us several valuable lessons:

- not to invest in individual companies,
- not to think we can time the market,
- not to chase big returns,
- not to place all our money in a single asset class,
- and not to invest in a single market sector.

When we returned from travel, I went to the library and read *The Financial Times Guide to Investing* by Glen Arnold and watched Pete Matthew's free videos at *meaningfulmoney.tv*. These great sources of information got the basics across to me: what shares, bonds and funds are, how they can earn us (or cost us) money, what fees are

The Non-Trepreneurs

involved and how experts try and guess future changes in stock values. From blogs like *jlcollinsnh.com* (and his book *The Simple Path to Wealth*), *madfientist.com* and *mrmoneymustache.com* I started to understand concepts like the Safe Withdrawal Rate (more on this soon) and how seemingly-small fees, say 1% a year, could create an enormous drag on our wealth over the years.

I discovered that many non-trepreneurs opted to invest in a specific type of fund (funds pool together shares in several companies), called an Exchange Traded Fund (ETF), and frequently from a company called Vanguard (*www.vanguardinvestor.co.uk*). They also tended to choose 'passive' rather than 'active' funds. To illustrate the difference let's look at the UK's FTSE 100, a logical collection (called an 'index') of the biggest 100 companies floated on the London Stock Exchange (*www.londonstockexchange.com*).

The Vanguard FTSE 100 (VUKE) passive index-tracking ETF buys shares in all 100 companies in the FTSE 100, weighted to match the relative value of each company in the index. When the FTSE 100 goes up, VUKE goes up by the same amount. When it falls, VUKE falls too. An active fund concentrating on large UK companies will, on the other hand, have a fund manager (and team) who try and guess which of those 100 company's shares will do better than the others, buying more of those shares and selling others to try to outperform the FTSE 100. For this additional effort, the active fund will charge higher fees.

Like the FSTE 100, the S&P 500 tracks the value of 500 large companies floated on stock exchanges in the US. Vanguard has a fund which tracks this index too (VUSA). Back in 2008 billionaire investor Warren Buffet made a one million dollar bet with Protégé Partners LLC[61] that their actively managed funds wouldn't

---

[61] *www.investopedia.com/articles/investing/030916/buffetts-bet-hedge-funds-year-eight-brka-brkb.asp*

beat the returns (after fees, costs and expenses) of a passive index tracking S&P 500 fund (like VUSA) over a decade period. Despite the markets crashing soon after the experiment started on 1 Jan 2008, the S&P 500 fund increased by 85.4% by 1 Jan 2018 (an average of 7.1% per year). Over the same time period, the five actively managed hedge funds increased by an average of only 22.0% (or 2.2% per year). None of the active funds beat the S&P 500 tracker, achieving between 2.9% and 62.8% total return over the decade.

Warren's passive fund clearly won. Arguably, Warren could have been lucky, another downturn before the end of the experiment could have handed the advantage back to the actively-managed hedge funds, but the result still stands: the high fees of the active funds meant that in this particular test they could not out-perform the low fee passive fund.

Our Shares Investments Journey

We started our share investing journey by opening a stocks and shares ISA for each of us, and a share dealing account with our bank. This didn't cost anything at the time, although the bank later introduced a quarterly fee for our trading accounts. They also charge a trading fee each time we buy or sell a fund, although we do this rarely, so the impact is relatively low.

The Money Saving Expert website has up to date reviews on the various stocks and shares ISA providers available and the amount they charge to open an ISA, manage it, trade, and transfer out of it:

www.moneysavingexpert.com/savings/stocks-shares-isas

They also indicate how many funds the ISA provides access to and the approximate management cost of those funds, but you need to check with the provider that your specific funds are available.

We had saved up £10,000 to invest which we split evenly between five different investments, four funds and shares in a single company, so we could learn how each of them performed over the coming years, and how we reacted as their values went up and down.

We chose the funds below. **Please let me reiterate, don't treat anything in this book as a recommendation for a specific fund or other type of investment.** We made sure that we read and understood each of these fund's Key Investor Information Documents before investing and did our research into what types of fund might work well for us. For example, we prefer to invest in *physical ETFs*, not *synthetic*, meaning they invest directly in shares rather than trading in derivatives, so we checked these all met that and a few other criteria.

- **Vanguard's FTSE 100 tracker ETF (VUKE)**, which invests in the largest 100 companies listed on the London Stock Exchange. This has the 'symbol' VUKE, which is a shorthand used when trading funds, tracking their value using Google Finance (*www.google.co.uk/finance*) and so on.
- **Vanguard's Standard & Poor's 500 ETF (VUSA)**, which invests in 500 large companies listed on stock exchanges in the USA. Note that there's no reason we UK-based investors have to invest in UK companies, although if we invest in companies listed abroad we have to take account of *currency risk*, the fact exchange rates with the pound could decrease the value of our funds.
- **Vanguard's High Dividend Yield ETF (VHYL)**, which invests in roughly 1,600 large and medium-sized companies, which tend to pay higher-than-average dividends.
- **Vanguard's All World ETF (VWRL)**, which invests in around 3,500 companies spread around the globe, large and mid-sized, in both developed and emerging markets.

One reason for choosing these funds was their low costs. Investment companies charge various fees for managing their funds. Some charge an entry fee, an ongoing annual fee, performance fees and exit fees. These are all seemingly small percentages, adding up to less than 2% say, but the long-term impact on wealth can be large.

The above Vanguard funds charge an ongoing annual fee of between around 0.07% and 0.25%, but have no entry, exit or performance fees. On a £10,000 portfolio, this means we'll pay between £7 and £25 for the first year in fund fees (this is automatically deducted from the quarterly dividend payments). For a fund which charges 1%, that would increase to £100 a year. The difference doesn't sound much, but over the long term, they are. Let's take two £10,000 investments, one in a fund which charges 0.2% a year, and one which charges 1% a year. Assuming both funds achieve a 7% annual return, the 0.2% fund would be worth £34,815 after 20 years, while the 1% charge fund would be worth £29,878, a £5,000 difference.

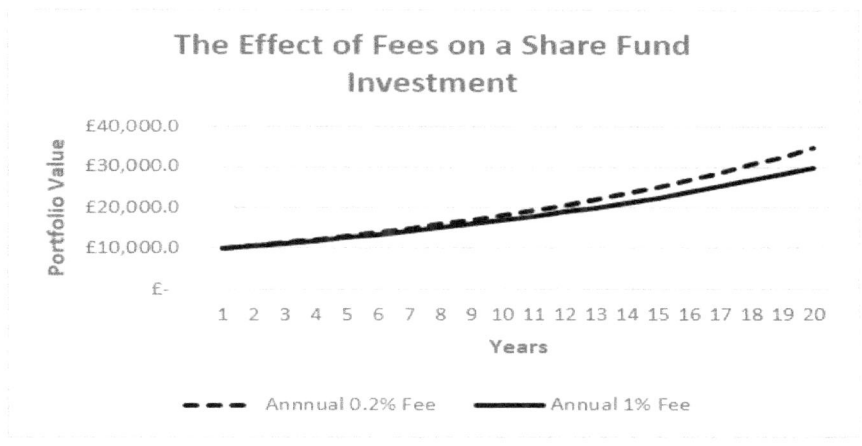

We were investing during a 'bull market' (when stock prices tend to rise, as opposed to a 'bear market' when they fall). We didn't know then that the bull would run for another six years until the 2020 COVID-19 crash.

Perhaps luckily for us the shares we bought in the single company crashed almost as soon as we bought them, losing 50% of their value in a matter of months, and were still worth 25% less than we paid for them when we sold them. This reminded us of the lesson we learned from the couple on our travels, that we were amateurs and didn't know how to value individual shares! We recognised we'd made a couple of mistakes:

- The shares had been appreciating sharply when we bought them, making us feel that we didn't want to miss out on this growth. It turned out this was just speculative buying rather than any underlying value increase in the business.
- We thought we knew the business and thought it offered a good product. These thoughts probably still hold true, but the market decides the price of shares, not what we think.

The index trackers have performed better, and we continued to invest in various Vanguard passive index funds during the bull market, before starting to simply buy VWRL for its simplicity and worldwide diversification.

As mentioned above, during the 2020 crash our portfolio value dropped 30%, testing our nerve. The temptation at this point was to sell and hold cash, then try and buy back at a lower point in the market, a seemingly obvious and simple strategy but very difficult to do in practice. We passed the test and didn't sell. Studies show this behaviour leads to much lower long-term returns as the tendency is to sell when prices have already fallen and buy back in when prices have risen past the point they were sold.

Our plan now is to steadily invest any savings we have into VWRL, re-investing dividends from the existing shares, keeping them inside our ISAs where possible. Our bank's share-trading platform doesn't have an option for automatic dividend re-investing, so we save up until we're able to invest £2,500 to £5,000 and do a trade at that point. Each trade costs us £10.50, a cost of between 0.42% and

0.21% of our investment. When we get access to our pensions, we may start to treat the dividends and capital gains as income and increase our lifestyle spending. That leads to the question of how much we can take from these funds without depleting them, which is where the safe withdrawal rate comes in.

When we sold our house, we were unable to buy shares entirely within our ISAs as the proceeds exceeded our ISA allowance (£20,000 each). Instead, we bought £40,000 worth of shares in our ISAs, and the rest in General Accounts (GAs). These GAs are subject to income and capital gains tax. However, the government allows us each to can earn £2,000 per year tax-free in dividends, and £12,300 a year each in capital gains. We're not likely to exceed either of these.

The Safe Withdrawal Rate (SWR)

One of the biggest questions non-trepreneurs must deal with is this: how much money do I need in investments to provide for my retirement income until I die? The answer comes in two halves:

1. Firstly, we need to understand how much money we spend each year and allow for it to increase with inflation or other foreseeable costs. By keeping the Household Balance Sheet (HBS) and Household Profit & Loss (HPL) we wrote about in Part 3, we have at least some of this information to hand.
2. Secondly, understanding how much income our investments are likely to generate over the coming decades.

This second point is where the Safe Withdrawal Rate (SWR) comes in. It is the percentage of money you can safely withdraw from your investments, so you don't run out of money before you die. The SWR is only applicable to paper assets, such as share and bond funds, as investment engines. It doesn't apply to commodities, rental property and so on.

Shares and share funds can generate income in two ways: by (hopefully) going up in value and by paying out dividends. Bonds and Bond Funds can do the same, although instead of dividends they pay out interest payments and they're likely to appreciate by less than shares (and fall less during bear markets). Neither shares nor bonds create a steady return, they're volatile and both their value and returns are likely to fluctuate significantly over the years and decades. History has shown us that some years share funds will lose value and in others they'll boom.

This variability in returns introduces the *sequence of return* risk, which is one reason working out how much we can take from our funds is problematic. Sequence of return risk tells us that the value of a portfolio in the earlier years of retirement matters more than in the later years.

As an example, let's say you have £500,000 in a share fund at the point you choose to stop working. You start by taking £20,000 a year in income from the fund, a 4% SWR (20/500 x 100). The income will probably come from a combination of dividends and selling some of your shares, with the expectation the remaining shares will appreciate enough to make up for their sale. You plan to increase this amount in line with inflation, so in year two, with 3% inflation you would take out £20,600, and then £21,218 in year 3 and so on.

If you're unlucky, the stock market might fall significantly just after you retire, cutting the value of your fund to £300,000. Any money you now take from the fund has a higher impact than before. Your £20,000 withdrawal would now represent 6.7% of your fund (20/300 x 100), way above the 4% SWR.

At the point you retired, your £500,000 fund had to increase by 7% to retain its real value, allowing for your 4% withdrawal and 3% inflation. However, because your £20,000 now represents 6.7% of your £300,000 fund, it now needs to increase by 9.7%. History tells us that a 9.7% increase is statistically much less likely to happen. So, if there's a major stock market drop your fund would probably depreciate much more quickly in the early years of your retirement.

In 1998, researchers at Trinity University in Texas[62] carried out a study called *Retirement Savings: Choosing a Withdrawal Rate That Is Sustainable*, nick-named the Trinity Study. The aim of the study was to try and calculate the best possible SWR, that being a SWR which had a statistically low chance of completely depleting a portfolio over retirements between 15 and 30 years long. In other words, how much can you spend each year without running out of money before you die. The researchers created a set of theoretical portfolios, each with a different proportion of shares and bonds, ranging from 100% shares to 100% bonds. They used historical data from the S&P 500 index for the shares, and assumed long-term, high-grade corporate bonds.

They simulated a series of 'retirements' for each portfolio, each starting in a different year covering two time periods (1925 to 1995 and 1946 to 1995). They re-ran the simulations with withdrawal rates between 3% and 12%. Importantly, they assumed:

- That the retiree wouldn't alter the amount they took each year, other than increasing it with inflation. If you can reduce your spending in years your portfolio performs poorly, then you increase the chances of not running out of money.
- They also didn't allow for fees in their calculations. With fund and platform fees totalling 0.5%, a 4% withdrawal rate really takes 4.5% from your fund, which increases the risk of it being depleted.

The study reported the probability for each share/bond mix of the fund lasting 15, 20, 25 or 30 years for each withdrawal rate. It also

---

[62] *www.aaii.com/files/pdf/6794_retirement-savings-choosing-a-withdrawal-rate-that-is-sustainable.pdf*

reported the average (mean), median, minimum and maximum values of the portfolios at the end of the retirement terms. In other words, it provided a lot of statistics! It doesn't just say 'take 4% from your fund and you'll be fine'. In my opinion it's important to read the report, understand the basis of the research and draw your own conclusions, but the authors had this to say:

"If history is any guide for the future, then withdrawal rates of 3% and 4% are extremely unlikely to exhaust any portfolio of stocks and bonds during any of the payout periods".

The study results were subsequently updated by the authors in 2011[63], concluding that the 4% SWR was still likely to be applicable.

This 4% SWR is the rule of thumb many FIRE bloggers work to when assessing the target amount of money they need in shares/bonds. That said, the SWR is very heavily debated! As our retirements could last for 40 or 50 years, the results of the Trinity Studies need to be treated with caution. Also, there's no guarantee the future share and bond markets will replicate the same historical patterns.

As a result, some non-trepreneurs opt for a 3.5% SWR, some for 3% and a few are pessimistic enough to drop all the way to 2% (with a nigh-on impossible chance of ever running out of money). As ever, there's risk in whichever path you choose. If you go for 4%, there's a higher risk of running out of money. If you go for 2%, there's a higher chance you'll work many more years than you needed to, to build up a much higher portfolio than required to meet your needs.

If you like, you can run your own version of the Trinity Study, using simulators like *firecalc.com* and *cfiresim.com* which give a visual idea of how your portfolio might perform. This can be especially useful if you are planning a retirement longer than 30 years, or if you want

---

[63] *www.bogleheads.org/wiki/Trinity_study_update*

to see how things change if you can be flexible about the amount of money you withdraw each year.

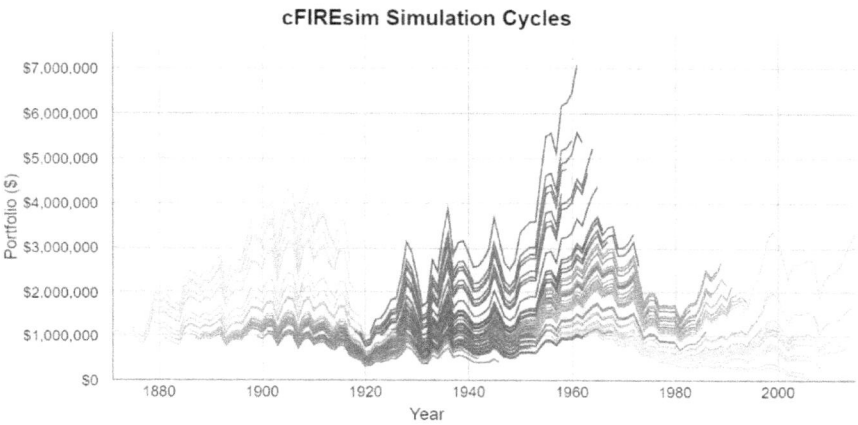

These results from cfiresim.com, show how a $1m starting portfolio would have performed historically with a 4% SWR over a 40-year period. Each line is a different starting year. This example assumes a 75%/25% share/bond mix, fees of 0.35%, and that the retirees can reduce their spending to $30,000 in poor market conditions. Under these conditions, the simulator shows that historically no early retiree would have run out of money, and many would have gotten much richer in retirement.

If you're still not comfortable, talk to a finance expert and get their advice. I'd personally go armed with at least a basic understanding of the underlying concepts: how shares, bonds, various types of fund and their associated fees work, and how your income and capital gains will be taxed.

Pensions

Julie and I were both given the option to pay into occupational pensions when we started working in our 20s. Our employers matched our contributions, up to a set percentage. The UK government gave us a tax advantage too, by deducting our pension contributions before calculating our income tax. We'll be taxed when we take the money out, but by deferring the tax in this way the pensions should grow to a higher value.

As the years went by, we individually kept up our pension payments, not really noticing them as we never saw the money in the first place (the *pay yourself first* tactic I mentioned earlier). It was automatically taken from our monthly pay and placed into whatever company's pension we worked for at the time. All we noticed was a letter every year from the pension company saying how much it was worth and how much it might pay out when we retired in our 60s, which felt like a lifetime away.

We could very easily have spent that money on something more fun. Why didn't we? I'm not sure. It was probably the offer of 'free money' from our employers which swung it for me. Whatever the reasons, we're very glad we paid into those pensions when we had the chance, as they now offer a great safety net for us.

In all we had seven personal pensions between us. We've moved all but one of them into SIPPs, self-invested personal pensions with AJ Bell. This allows us full control over what they are invested in, gives us the option to start taking an income from them when we're 55, and has lowered the fees we pay to run the pensions. We've currently got them invested in Vanguard's All World fund, VWRL and have them set up to automatically re-invest dividends.

Our remaining pension is a final salary pension, a type of Defined Benefits (DB) pension. These are seen as the gold standard for pensions, however most companies stopped allowing new people to join them, offering Defined Contribution (DC) pensions instead. The DB pension has the benefit of paying out a pre-defined, fixed amount each year in retirement, increasing with inflation (up to a point). This lack of volatility is a major benefit of this kind of pension. However, final salary pensions aren't subject to the same kinds of flexibility as DC pensions. Instead of being able to take an income from age 55, we must wait until I'm 63 before we're able to touch it. Also, we can't do anything about the way the pension is invested: that's all hidden from us, which is arguably a good thing for many people. Finally, if I die Julie only gets about ⅔ the annual pension, and if we both die, there is nothing we can leave to any beneficiaries of our estate.

Every 12 months we're able to request (for free) a transfer value for this pension, indicating how much it would be worth in cash if we choose to transfer it to a SIPP. Legally, as the pension is worth over £30,000, we'd need to pay for formal advice from an independent financial advisor (IFA) before we could carry out the transfer, and in our experience few IFAs are willing to offer this service. We've opted to just leave this pension as it is for now, and will review it when I'm 55.

We're also eligible for the UK state pension when we're 67. Future legislation changes could delay that age, or even shift to a partly or fully means-tested model, meaning we might not receive any state pension. While there are no guarantees, it seems very unlikely the state pension will be completely abolished, as too many people would be impoverished in old age. We think of the state pension as a further safety net in case we experience serious unforeseen money problems in the coming decades.

There's a government website which enables you to see how much state pension you may get (based on current legislation), and how many remaining years of National Insurance Contributions (NICs) you need to buy to get the maximum amount: *www.gov.uk/check-state-pension*.

While we were working full-time our employers paid our NICs as part of our PAYE (Pay As You Earn) salary. Once we finished work, those payments stopped and when I was working as a contractor, I was responsible for paying my NICs through my tax return. Because we stopped working early, Julie and I are quite a few years short of the 35 years of contributions which would entitle us to the maximum state pension. So, we're currently buying additional years of NICs, again through our self-assessment tax returns.

We're classed as self-employed these days and run our blog and book sales income through a partnership company, which allows us to buy Class 2 NICs. This is a relatively cheap gamble against us not being eligible for the state pension under future law. Even if Class 2 NICs are abolished (the government has indicated this might happen) then the more expensive Class 3 NICs are still good value, assuming we survive for more than a few years after state pension age (we used a spreadsheet to work this out).

If we both pay for a full contribution record (35 qualifying years) and are still eligible at our state pension age, we'll receive around £15,000 of taxable income a year between us. That's in today's money, again depending on legislation it will hopefully increase in line with inflation.

Our Net Worth and Asset Allocation

While it's always interesting to peek into someone else's finances, probably because the subject is almost a taboo here in the UK, our net worth won't be of much use to you, or anyone other than us. I can't emphasise enough that you need to know your own numbers. The amount you need will be completely personal to you. You'll have to work out how much income you need to live a good, free life, and how much in investments you'll need to produce it.

That's said, I've put our own net worth and asset allocation details in here as an example, because I want to show you what financial independence could look like. When we quit work in 2015, our net worth was roughly £700,000. Since then it's increased to around £1.2m. The value of our houses and shares have increased, and I worked a four-month contract at one point which added to our wealth (I don't intend to repeat that). We've created new income streams from our books, blog and a network marketing side gig. We have continued to live below our means, enabling us to continue saving. Despite our best efforts to spend money, last year we still spent almost £11,000 less than we earned, so we invested that money into our share funds. Weirdly, we're 'retired' but getting wealthier.

Our net worth is split across these assets:

Asset	Type	Percentage
2 Bed Bungalow	Real Estate	9%
4 Bed House & Shop	Real Estate	15%
Cash	Cash	1%
Premium Bonds	Government Bonds	5%
ISA Share Funds	Shares	16%
GA Share Funds	Shares	15%
SIPPs	Pension (Shares)	17%
Final Salary Pension	Pension	20%
Motorhome & Car	Depreciating Vehicles	2%

Here are some explanatory notes on the above:

- We're currently living on income from around 50% of our income-generating assets (rental income from properties and solar panel payments). We'll take income from the remaining 50% as we age (most of this will become accessible in our mid-50s to mid-60s).
- 97% of our net worth is invested in appreciating, cash-generating assets. This is very high, since we include our main home as we let out the bedrooms and the shop embedded in it.
- The bungalow and house with shop both have solar PV panels on the roofs. These cost a total of around £10,000 to install. We haven't added this to the market value of the properties, as we can't be sure these installations increased their worth.

The Non-Trepreneurs

- We have relatively few personal belongings of worth, having sold or given them away, so have only included our motorhome and car in this table.
- We don't include anything in our net worth calculation for the state pension, inheritance or any other potential windfalls.

Other Non-Trepreneur Investments

Although Julie and I invest in the same types of asset most non-trepreneurs opt for, these aren't the only options available. This section briefly looks at some of the other approaches taken.

Real Estate Investment Trusts

A REIT is a type of fund which owns, operates or finances income-generating residential and/or commercial property. They provide a way to invest in the housing market, for example, avoiding many of the problems involved in physically owning buy-to-let properties. Some REITs own physical property, while others buy shares in real estate companies and other REITs. REITs produce income for shareholders in the form of dividends.

Dividend Stocks

Some companies have a history of paying out high dividends, typically generating a yield of between 3% and 5%. The idea behind dividend investing is to buy stocks in just those companies you believe will pay out a good dividend in the coming year.

One dividend strategy, called *The Dogs of the Dow*, proposes placing an equal amount in the 10 highest dividend-paying stocks in the Dow Jones Index each year[64]. In theory you can generate all your 'retirement' income from dividends, avoiding having to sell any shares for income.

---

[64] *www.dogsofthedow.com*

Dividends aren't guaranteed to continue of course. In the event of a financial or other crisis, affected companies can completely stop paying dividends out to shareholders. Also, the value of the shares you own could go down, potentially leading to a higher loss than the income you receive from dividends.

Peer-to-Peer Lending (P2P)
Internet platforms enable you to act like a bank, lending money out to individuals and businesses in the form of interest-paying loans. Some UK examples include Ratesetter (*www.ratesetter.com*), Funding Circle (*www.fundingcircle.com*) and Zopa (*www.zopa.com*).

Back in 2014, Pete Adeney (*www.mrmoneymustache.com*) reported on a peer-to-peer lending experiment he'd been running using a US-based platform. He later updated the results, showing he'd started off with annual returns of over 20% in 2012 but the returns gradually dropped off until his balance had started to fall in 2016 and he later opted to withdraw all his money from the platform.

Pete's is the only 'mainstream' FIRE blog I've come across who has tried P2P lending, but there are plenty of smaller, less established bloggers writing about it (search for 'FIRE P2P UK blog'). P2P lending offers potentially high returns but carries risks which Julie and I aren't personally comfortable with, the biggest being the potential for the P2P platform to financially fail, seeing us losing all our investment. P2P lending just doesn't fit our risk profile.

Owning Gold
In his book *How to Own the World*, Andrew Craig makes the case for including gold in your portfolio of investments. Gold (and other commodities) don't generate a cash income. Instead, the investing aim is to increase the value of the gold you own before you sell it. Indeed, looking at *bullionvault.com*, gold was trading at about £6,000 per kilogram in 2001, and was worth £47,500 per kilogram in October 2020, an 11% cumulative annual return. Over the same time

period, the US Standard & Poor's 500 index generated a 6.5% annual return with dividends re-invested[65].

We haven't invested in gold mainly because (a) we're looking for a cash return without needing to sell any assets and (b) we don't claim to understand what drives its value up and down.

Cryptocurrency

Cryptocurrencies have been mentioned more often within the FIRE community, but remain a fringe asset compared with shares, bonds and real estate. The idea with crypto is to buy them, and sell later with the aim of making a profit.

While I have an understanding of the underlying technology involved, I have no understanding of what drives the value of these currencies, other than speculative buying, and we've never invested in any of them. That's not to say they aren't a way to make money. Even though Bitcoin lost around 70% of its value between Nov 2021 and July 2022, anyone who had invested in it in early 2019 would still have increased the value of their asset five times over.

Taxes

Neither of us are qualified to give tax advice; please treat this information accordingly! I've briefly touched on taxes a few times earlier in the book, but they're important enough for their own section. Taxation can make some forms of investment far more profitable than others, and it's worth spending time understanding tax when building or refreshing your financial independence plan.

Income Tax

Under the current UK tax law, income tax is levied on a tiered system. Everyone gets a *personal allowance,* an amount they can earn without paying any tax. Above that they start to pay increasingly

---

[65] *dqydj.com/sp-500-return-calculator*

higher percentages depending on how much they earn. The rates applicable here in England in 2022/2023 are shown below (*www.gov.uk/income-tax-rates*).

Band	Taxable Income	Tax Rate
Personal Allowance	Up to £12,570	0%
Basic Rate	£12,571 to £50,270	20%
Higher Rate	£50,271 to £150,000	40%
Additional Rate	over £150,000	45%

For Julie and I, it makes sense for us to split our income evenly to make the most of our personal allowances. Also, not all income is counted in the *taxable income* amount. Capital gains, interest and dividends from assets in an ISA aren't taxable for example, see:

www.gov.uk/individual-savings-accounts/how-isas-work

Tax planning will start to become more important for us in the coming years, as we're already starting to exceed our personal allowances. Once our pensions start to become available, it makes sense to shield as much income as we can inside our ISAs. For us, this has meant selling rental property and moving the money into ETFs. It will now take several years to completely move the money from our General Accounts (GAs) into stocks and shares ISAs, as there is currently a £20,000 a year limit per person.

We pay income tax (and national insurance) through self-assessment tax returns each year, as we don't pay tax through PAYE (*www.gov.uk/self-assessment-tax-returns*). When the tax situation is complicated, like when I was self-employed under a limited company, we employ an accountant to help us complete these returns and any other formal reporting required.

Capital Gains Tax (CGT)

As mentioned above, capital gains aren't taxed on assets held in an ISA, but any gains we make on our rental houses will be subject to CGT. As of 2022 we can make a gain of £12,300 per person, each year, before paying any CGT (the latest amount is here: *www.gov.uk/capital-gains-tax*). CGT is another driver for us to sell our rental properties and move the money into ISA-shielded shares and bonds.

In Summary

It would be exceptionally difficult for us to save up enough capital as cash to enable us to stop working decades before normal retirement age. By investing we're able to use a smaller amount of capital to generate various income streams for us, which fund our early retirement.

As a rule, non-trepreneurs use rental property, stocks and bonds (the latter two normally in the form of funds) to make them financially free. Property generates monthly rent, stocks pay out dividends and bonds pay coupons (or interest). Hopefully they'll each also appreciate, so can be sold (or partially sold) for a profit.

If you're anything like us, investing won't come naturally. We spent lots of time reading books and blogs and watching videos to understand how investing at a personal level works, before we started to deliberately invest. I once saw this described as roughly the same level of effort as learning to drive, and that rings true to me (although I did fail my driving test twice!).

Once you do start to invest, you should find that by re-investing the cash generated you can gradually, spiral your wealth upwards, compounding it over the years. Eventually you'll reach a point where your investment income meets all your expenditure, at which point you're free of the need for a job, you're financially independent and the world is your oyster.

Part Seven: Seeking Balance

"People have enough to live by but nothing to live for; they have the means but no meaning."

Viktor Frankl, Psychiatrist and Holocaust Survivor

Stepping aside from office politics, awkward bosses and the long lines of commuting brake lights has undoubtably increased my quality of life. But it would be untrue for me to say that freedom from work alone has proved the key to ever-lasting happiness.

It's a great position to be in, to be free of the pressing and ever-present need to earn money. But achieving financial independence isn't worth it *at all costs*, nor is it the pinnacle of life. It's just a new starting point, in my experience, and it makes sense to prepare yourself during the build-up for the phases which come afterwards.

This part of the book looks at how we're trying to find ongoing meaning and balance throughout our lives. It also tries to address some of the criticisms of the non-trepreneur approach to life.

What Makes A Good Life?

It seems to me that a good life is based on a few simple things:

- Loving relationships.
- Contributing (giving).
- A sense of personal progression.

We need money to avoid the grinding hopelessness of poverty. Once we've enough to meet our basic needs though, my personal view is that love, giving and progression quickly rise to the very top of our requirements for a good life. There's little point in being financially independent if it makes us unhappy, by failing to integrate these important elements into our lives.

Loving Relationships

A multi-generational study being carried out by Harvard University in the US has found that roughly 50% of our happiness comes from our genes: if our parents were content, we're more likely to be too[66]. Not much we can do about our genes. The rest is under our control though, and the greatest single factor which influences that happiness is the warmth of our relationships with others. Not money or fame, but how well we get on with those around us, how close we are to people.

If you've never come across *ted.com* (TED stands for Technology, Entertainment and Design) then I strongly recommend having a look at the free talks it hosts. One focuses on the above study, titled *What Makes a Good Life? Lessons from the Longest Study on Happiness* by Robert Waldinger and is well worth a few minutes of your time. Robert makes another significant point about the study results: better relationships and more social connection also equate to improved health and longevity.

Another influence for me is Viktor Frankl's book, *Man's Search for Meaning*. Viktor was Jewish and survived the holocaust, enduring the most inhumane conditions possible in several concentration camps. His book is deeply insightful and moving. In living through conditions which stripped away almost all superficial meaning from his life and his fellow prisoners, he could see the true meaning. In a book packed with insight, these themes stood out for me:

- Love is the ultimate and highest goal.
- Meaning is unique to each of us, and each moment in time.
- It's our personal responsibility to find meaning in our lives.

---

[66] *en.wikipedia.org/wiki/Grant_Study*

Contribution

We only get what we give. If we're unwilling to give love, we're unlikely to receive it. If we won't give our time to others, they're unlikely to give theirs to us. If we don't want to take on big hairy challenges, the world's not likely to gift us big hairy rewards.

Everyone's sense of personal contribution will differ. I had a feeling of guilt when we quit work that I didn't quickly find myself wanting to go out and volunteer. Julie and I have given our time in perhaps less obvious ways, spending thousands of hours working on our travel blog, responding to questions and offering encouragement. This is a win-win for us. We get a great feeling when someone writes to say our blog has helped them. Sometimes our readers choose to buy one of our motorhome travel books, which generates a financial reward for us too.

Only in the last year have we started to volunteer in other ways, helping our local running club. My feeling is we'll give more and more of our time as the years pass, but that this should be a natural progression and not something forced through guilt.

Progression

A friend of ours, who acted as a catalyst for us in altering the course of our lives, has a saying that *"man is a goal-getting animal"*. Tony Robbins, American author and life coach, has a similar view on human happiness: *"While achievements and material things may excite you for the moment, the only thing that's going to make you happy long-term is knowing that you're making progress."*

This rings true for me. I loved the chase to reach financial independence but neglected to put in place a plan for what I'd do with the decades which followed. I'd missed the critical need we all have for a sense of progression, of improvement in life. For much of my adult life I'd gotten this sensation from a faster motorbike, a bigger house, career promotions or a flashier smart phone. I still attach a sense of progression to some of these things, but it's in a much smaller way now.

As I write this, I realise that finding ongoing sources of progression is an even bigger challenge than contribution. There are a series of 'obvious' areas I could focus on: writing, learning a musical instrument, getting fitter, learning a foreign language for example. I've tried all of these and only writing and athletics have stuck, the others haven't. Some of this is probably laziness, but I've found what motivates me is personal to me, it can't be imposed by other people's ideas of what we should do, that just doesn't work.

While I used to run in my 20s, I stopped well before my 30s. It was only a couple of years after hitting financial independence that I started again, aged 45 and weighing 20Kg (over 3 stone) heavier. I was prompted to train because Julie had started running for her mental health, and I also found I needed the challenge in my life.

Since then I've run a marathon, a few ultra-marathons (over 26.2 miles) and have improved my shorter distance race times. I'm nowhere near as fast as I was in my 20s, but I can still compete against those in my age bracket. The mindset I needed to gain financial independence has many similarities to the mindset that I needed for my running training:

- I needed to develop self-belief that I could attain a goal that most people around me will not manage or want to achieve.
- I had to train consistently over a long period of time, ideally several years.
- I needed to voluntarily give up some comfort now, in return for a reward in the future.
- I needed to adopt a holistic approach to life. Heavy drinking and eating fast food won't help with marathon running in the same way impulse buying won't help getting financially free.

- I needed to research and follow strategies adopted by those who came before me.

My running training even prompted me to give up alcohol about four years ago, and to work towards a more balanced diet. I now weigh 73kg, train 5 or 6 times a week and have completed multiple ultra-marathons, including two 50-mile runs. Both running and book writing give me a sense of progression, of tackling challenges and achieving goals that I found was missing in my life once we'd reached financial independence.

Running the Zermatt Ultramarathon, Matterhorn in the background

Comfort & Discomfort

After returning from a multi-month motorhome tour, I turn on the water tap at home to take a shower, or press the button to flush the loo, and I'm grateful for just how convenient these things are. Our motorhome has a 100-litre fresh-water tank which lasts the two of us several days. Back home, the average shower gets through about 60 litres, so at the same rate our tank would be empty in a single day, even without drinking any of it or washing pots. The loo in most European motorhomes is cassette: a plastic box which fills up and must be carried to disposal point. Being able to simply push that button on the loo at home feels like a luxury!

The feeling only lasts a few days though, and we soon slip back into taking these modern-day luxuries for granted. The same goes for much of life. We heat our home using a wood burner, and the rooms are cool when we wake up in the morning. The warmth we get from an evening fire is enjoyed all the more. We know going for a fast run is going to be uncomfortable, but once we're home and have our breath back, we feel good about ourselves.

The point I'm trying to make is we need some discomfort in order to recognise and be more grateful for our comfort. This is very helpful in maintaining our low-cost lifestyle. By introducing some level of discomfort on purpose, we're continually grateful for what comforts we have. We may not be able to afford to buy a new car and replace it every couple of years, but we can afford to eat what we like, clothe ourselves, keep warm, buy luxury gadgets, take months-long trips, buy books and eat out from time to time. We're very grateful for what we have.

Work Life

I don't need to work for money anymore, but I still choose to. Why is that? Well, I write when I want to, on whatever topics I want and as much or as little as I like. I enjoyed writing this book, for example, spending maybe two or three hours a day on it. The rest of the time I spend cooking, exercising, reading, watching TV or listening to music.

Back in my corporate life I felt trapped by work. My job was secure, the company had lots of opportunities and I was paid very well. I still didn't enjoy it. I've tried to analyse why over the years, and I think it comes down to some combination of:

- **Value Conflicts**. I was being asked to spend a great deal of money on projects which had no measurements in place and, in my opinion, would certainly fail to create value, wasting money and also the time and energy of everyone involved.
- **Boredom**. Many IT projects were very much like ones I'd done before and didn't challenge me.
- **Negativity**. There was a general air of cynicism among some of my co-workers, which I found hard to shake off.
- **Imposter Syndrome**. The higher I climbed in my career, the more I felt I wasn't good enough to be where I was. My confidence was low as a result, which pushed up my stress levels.
- **Lack of Flexibility**. There was no option to take breaks from work longer than a couple of weeks, and holidays had to be booked way in advance to fit around colleagues so you couldn't always have time off when you wanted it.

Work provides security, income, structure, companionship, a sense of meaning and an ongoing challenge but it can also be a huge life constraint and source of stress. The key, I'm told, is to find a job which I enjoy so much it doesn't feel like work. Perhaps I've finally found it, writing books and blog posts on subjects which interest me, free of pressure.

Ownership & Agility

Julie and I have sold and given away a large percentage of our possessions over the past decade. Stuff is useful though. It's nice to own stuff. Life wouldn't be much fun without clothes, cooking pans or a seat to sit on! But there's truth in the saying that if you're not careful, your stuff can start to own you. It takes up emotional energy worrying about whether it's been nicked, lost or damaged. It creates inertia when it comes to thoughts about moving house or using a room or garage for another purpose. It refuses to go away when you finally decide you want rid of it, claiming it's too valuable or it might come in handy one day!

Buying stuff gives us a buzz. Carrying the branded bags home or unboxing the latest gadget feels good, it's exciting. For a while anyway, after which we'll be needing another hit as the euphoria dies away. Julie tells me she got over her need for a buying buzz when she found out how little value most of our stuff had when we sold it second hand, it really put her off buying things that she felt she didn't need. Her other approach came from knowing that while we are on the road our current average daily spend is £40.26 a day (yep, that's the level of details she tracks to). She asks herself if whatever she is looking at buying will bring her as much joy as a day of freedom on the road. Usually the answer is no, and the stuff is admired in the shop but left there.

While we're in our motorhome we've limited access to stuff. For two years we travelled without a TV and we shared a Kindle and a single smartphone. Our wardrobe is divided into shelves, and we have one each plus a small cupboard which has all our year-round, all-season clothes. You get the picture: we aren't backpacking or training as Buddhist monks, but compared to the contents of a three-bed house, we live with few possessions.

How does this feel? It feels wonderful! We have everything we need. The biggest purchases we've made on the road have been a corkscrew, when we broke ours after too much wine bottle opening, and a potato masher, which are surprisingly hard to find in Italy.

I'm not suggesting you fling all your stuff out onto the lawn, but just to consider how much agility are you giving up in return for owning it all? How might life feel if you were free of some of it?

Thrift
The non-trepreneur approach to getting financially-free requires very different thinking and actions to the norm. It's not a *normal*

thing to spend only 50% of your income, and anyone attempting it might well be perceived as being *tight* or a *penny pincher*. None of our friends and family feel this about us, we've chatted with them about it, but a journalist for a national newspaper wrote an article saying we make 'Scrooge look like a shopaholic'!

The headline came about because when we were interviewed for the article, we mentioned that we had agreed with our families and friends not to buy each other presents at Christmas. As we're all adults, we were buying stuff because it was expected, and if we're honest about it, it was stuff the other person probably didn't want or need. When we broached the idea with our loved ones, everyone welcomed the reduced stress of one less present to buy.

From our perspective we're just being careful with our money, making efficient, frugal use of it and getting the most 'bang for our buck'. Frugality becomes ingrained after a while, a fixed habit which, even if we were to be given a huge Premium Bond win, would be hard to lose.

I don't think of myself as a Scrooge-like character, as I'm not interested in acquiring more money. I'm keen to help our early retirement plan work, but if I were a real wonga-hoarder, I'd start looking for work tomorrow. Even with my rusty skills I could earn another few hundred thousand by the time I hit 'normal' retirement age. I prefer my freedom though, and if that requires a bit of penny pinching from time to time, so be it.

In Summary

There's no point getting financially-free if you're miserable as a result. Life involves balance, and each of us will find that balance in different ways. Some of us need to spend more than others to meet our needs. Some will need more space to live in. Some will be comfortable sat at the beach, while others need the dynamism and energy of a fast-moving work environment.

The Non-Trepreneurs

I found that tipping into early retirement freed me of much of the frustration and anxiety I felt with my office job, particularly with the bureaucracy involved. The anxiety came back after a couple of years though, revealing that it wasn't completely caused by work. To manage it I had to spend time looking at how I could better balance my life. I gave up alcohol, focussed more on running, started to grasp the opportunities provided by writing blog posts and books and accepted that life is an ongoing challenge. Getting financially-free was just the start.

Part Eight: The Reality of (Very) Early Retirement

"The purpose of life is to live it, to taste experience to the utmost, to reach out eagerly and without fear for newer and richer experience."

Eleanor Roosevelt, First Lady of the United States

In my corporate career I felt frustrated that I was spending so much of my time either sat in traffic or sat behind a desk, pushing electronic paper. I sensed my life ebbing away, all the while too fearful to risk my income and lifestyle. Like many of us, it took a crisis to shove me sideways out of this dark groove, in my case increasing anxiety, chest pains and a sense of depression, of my sanity starting to slip.

After a frank talk with Julie, one of those life-defining moments, we chose to leave work and travel, living from savings we'd built up. That turning point set us off on a period of several years of travel, fighting for financial independence and yet more travel. Now, years later, we've been through some interesting, unexpected mental cycles. It's become clearer what our lives are about, although filling the days remains an ongoing challenge, but a nice one to have!

Stepping into the Blinding Light

After our two-year career break, as we turned 40, we felt we'd a choice to make. We could go back into higher-pressure jobs which we didn't enjoy or take a lower-stress path into jobs which made us fulfilled but didn't pay as well. Once we'd understood the possibility of financial independence, we effectively opted to 'sacrifice' a few years of life to earn and invest as much as possible as quickly as possible.

We knew that if this worked, it would free us from mandatory work forever. This idea fired us up, me in particular, and working 60 or 70 hours a week became our norm for a couple of years. I described the sensation as a blinding light I could strive towards with everything I had. We sat behind computers during the day and renovated a house at night and weekends.

When we decided to rent out rooms in that house the tipping point, when our income would exceed our expenses, came forward rapidly. For many people this point, when you can leave work if you want to, retreats into the distance, something known as 'one more year syndrome'. The fear of having got the sums wrong, or maybe deciding an increased standard of retirement living is needed, pushes folks to keep working more and more years.

We didn't have this challenge. We had already decided that we would earn additional income once we had 'retired' if we needed it, somehow. By this point the relentless effort combined with a simple lack of fun had started to crush Julie and she was suffering with depression. The job she'd taken after returning from travel was misaligned with her values, so after another life-defining heart to heart chat, she left work and concentrated on getting the shop and house refurbishment completed. During that chat we looked at our numbers again and were able to work out how much longer it would take us to reach financial independence if she left work. As we were so close to the tipping point, it really helped her to make that difficult decision. With help from NHS counsellors, and recognition from me that we were pushing too hard, she thankfully came out the other side.

When I came to hand my notice in, my employer offered me more money to stay. We didn't get into numbers, as they were already paying me a high day rate, and a higher one wasn't going to change my mind. I worked a notice period to hand over my work and a friend who worked for the same company took a photo of me on the last day I left the office. I recall sensing euphoria for a moment. We'd already bought another motorhome, and within a couple of weeks set off on an 18-month adventure.

Job done, leaving the office for ever!

Shedding Guilt

To what extent are we conditioned to believe certain life-truths, like the fact we must work 9 to 5 for the forty healthiest years of our lives? I came to find out whenever we broke away from this 'standard path'.

In those initial months after leaving the office, mixed in with the feelings of elation and liberty was a strong sensation of guilt. It was an unconscious thing. Come Monday morning my mind sensed I should be at work, not walking along a beach or a mountain path. Social media reinforced this message by steadily reminding me of the norms I'd left behind. Whenever we spent time at home in the

UK, it didn't feel right that I was so free to do what I liked during the week, when my friends and ex-colleagues were still working.

It took maybe two years for the guilt to leak away from me. Julie didn't have anything like the same sensations. She saw it more clearly, I think. She felt that we'd worked hard, focussed our energy, thought about how we wanted to live, assessed the risks and taken the action needed to enable this new way of life. We deserved it.

Roughly around the same point the guilt eased away we found ourselves the subjects of media attention, featuring (very briefly) on a Channel 4 programme about retiring at 40. The programme was pretty poor, not really taking a serious look at the challenges involved, but it lead to us being featured in the Daily Mail and subsequently in a short video about early retirement which hit the front page of the BBC website in the UK, generating almost a million views. Both the Daily Mail website and the BBC's Facebook page allow their millions of followers to post comments about their articles and videos. As these streamed in, my eyes were opened.

I spent my formative years on a council estate and later in a terraced house on a street of miners and factory workers. I'm not naïve when it comes to the fact useful or hard work doesn't necessarily translate into high income. The most critical occupations are frequently among the lowest paid: bin men, nurses, cleaners, cooks, waitresses, delivery drivers. Getting financially independent in your 40s or 50s in one of the lower-paid jobs is, in my opinion, exceptionally difficult. I wouldn't argue with any of the comments which made this point.

What did come as a surprise to me how many people were willing to judge our personalities based on practically no information about us. The video posted by the BBC was barely two minutes long with little detail, yet hundreds of people felt the need to express their opinions of us. It served to teach us that the subject of money is, and always will be, attached to strong and sometimes destructive emotions: jealousy, shame, fear, anger. Since then we've been asked to take part in other TV, radio and newspaper features, but have politely declined.

Losing an Identity

I only picked up books about retirement after I'd retired. It would have made much more sense to read one or two of them beforehand, as the emotional process I went through is unsurprisingly common. Our identity, the sense of who we are in the world, is often strongly tied in with the work we do. When meeting new people, 'what is your name?' and 'what do you do?' are usually some of the first questions asked of us.

I spent my days at work understanding IT concepts and systems, talking to managers to understand what their business needed from us and drawing up designs, implementation plans, risk analyses, budgets, progress reports and so on. Once I left work, I stopped doing any of this. I (almost) completely lost interest in IT. My identity, it seemed, wasn't associated with computer systems, or I'd have carried on with it outside of formal, structure work. So who was I?

To start off with I identified myself as a 'financially-independent traveller and blogger', neither of us could bring ourselves to use the term 'retired'. We travelled widely, enjoying taking photos and creating videos, and writing about the places we visited, their history, the food we ate, people we met and whatever else befell us. After a year or so (making three years of full-time travel in a five-year period), I started to sense this wasn't all there was to life.

I'd unwittingly hit the dual walls of progression and contribution. The beaches, towns, castles, campsites, mountains, museums and restaurants were starting to merge into one. I'd spent years reading about all the places we visited, and didn't feel like I was learning anything new, I wasn't progressing mentally. I started to struggle

The Non-Trepreneurs

with anxiety as a result. Our goal of financial independence was to enable us to travel whenever and wherever we wanted. We never thought to ask ourselves – what we would do next.

Bouncing Back into Work

Going back to a day job isn't all that uncommon among early-retired non-trepreneurs. Jacob Fisker, author of the *Early Retirement Extreme* blog and book came out of retirement to work as a trader and researcher (he retired again four years later[67]). He wrote his reasons on his blog[68], talking mainly about how he missed the challenge of difficult problems, and he felt this new job would fill that need. It sounded to me that Jacob was missing the sense of progression we all need.

Sam Dogen, author of the *Financial Samurai* blog, indicated in 2019 that he planned to go back to work[69]. Sam's reasons for returning to work included wanting a break after two years of being a stay-at-home dad, more engagement with people through access to work colleagues and earning more money. Sam runs his blog as a business, an entrepreneur in retirement, although he and his wife have a net worth at least $3m (he stopped reporting it after 2012, but has since indicated that it has roughly doubled up to now).

When an opportunity came up for me to go back to work on a freelance (contract) basis, I decided to take it. Why? Firstly, it was the easy option, as I was struggling to work out how to attain a sense of both progression and contribution in early retirement. Secondly the money was good. Why would I care about this when we'd already retired? Because no matter how simple the 4% rule is,

---

[67] *www.getrichslowly.org/early-retirement-extreme*
[68] *earlyretirementextreme.com/so-long-and-thanks-for-all-the-fish.html*
[69] *www.financialsamurai.com/thinking-about-taking-a-vacation-by-going-back-to-full-time-work*

it's still difficult to know when enough is enough, the dreaded *one more year syndrome*.

My experience of the workplace was, however, short-lived. I went back to part of the company I'd left two years earlier. The culture was the same, colleagues were just as unhappy, prompting me to have to keep my mouth closed as they talked about the brand-new cars they had ordered or their latest gadget. The need for me to fly to another country to attend a one-hour meeting, or even worse to just be seen at a desk, was totally against my values and a waste of the Earth's resources.

My initial contract was for three months, which should have been long enough to get the work package completed, but it became clear it was going to take maybe a year, as progress was so slow in other parts of the project. Coming towards the end of my three-month contract Julie drew up a chart so I could mark each day out of 5 based on how good it made me feel. Needless to say, the scores weren't very high, so I stayed for one more month to handover to a replacement, and then I left. I've not been tempted to go back.

The Entrepreneur Opportunity

While being non-trepreneurs has enabled us to evade the need for fifty year working lives, this approach doesn't solve the subsequent problem: what to do with the endless hours freed up as a result. It came as an interesting surprise to us that one answer to this latter question was to finally become entrepreneurs.

Hopefully, we're in the early years of our financially-free lives, and we're equally new at being entrepreneurs. This transition happened to us largely by accident (much like our earlier shift from consumer-employees to non-trepreneurs). Our travel blog generated an opportunity to write and self-publish books on motorhome travel, and we currently earn around £6,000 a year running this publishing business.

Writing provides a solution to the twin problems of progression and contribution. Only when we decide to write about a specific subject do we realise how much we've learned generally during our time away from work, but also how little we know about certain aspects, forcing us to read and learn. Being able to summarise years of experience (good and bad) and pass it on to others who are in earlier positions on the same path has proven to build a solid sense of contribution to the world around us.

Ongoing Risks

There is no guarantee that says: *"you've hit your retirement target, you're 100% certain to have enough to live on, forever"*. Julie and I can't say for sure that we've 'done it', that we've amassed enough investments to never have to work again. I don't think anyone in their 40s can really say this, the retirement timescales are too long and too many things might happen, such as:

- **Divorce.** Our expenses are low as we share most costs. If we divorced and had to pay for two separate houses, for example, then our work-free lifestyles would be threatened. Having been out of the workforce for several years, we might be forced to look for relatively low-paid work to make ends meet.
- **Illness.** There is no guarantee that the UK's NHS will provide us with free-to-use healthcare throughout our lives. We may be forced to buy health insurance as we age, which could threaten to exceed our budget.
- **Underperforming investments.** We could make an error with our investments or they could simply underperform our expectations. We've deliberately diversified our money across various income streams to try and mitigate this risk. The best we can do here is to keep an eye on them and be prepared to change things around if necessary.
- **Something Unforeseen.** By definition, we don't know what this is!

Part Eight: The Reality of (Very) Early Retirement

We've spent years thinking about, reading up on and practising this lifestyle choice we just have to accept that something out-of-the-blue could scupper our plans. That's life. By keeping an eye on all our numbers, income, expenses and investment returns, we should spot any warning signs of problems early.

We also make sure we check in with each other every week, making time to really talk to each other and express our feelings. We've learned this is essential to keep our relationship on-track, whatever our finances might be doing.

Ongoing Wealth Management

Earlier in the book we looked at the way in which we track our finances, using a Household Balance Sheet (HBS) and a Household Profit & Loss Account (HPL). In our case these are spreadsheets which keep a record of everything we owe and own, and all our spending and income, to the penny. We also have these set up to feed into a dashboard view with graphs giving a quick view of how much cash we have, how much we're under (or over) spending against a target and so on.

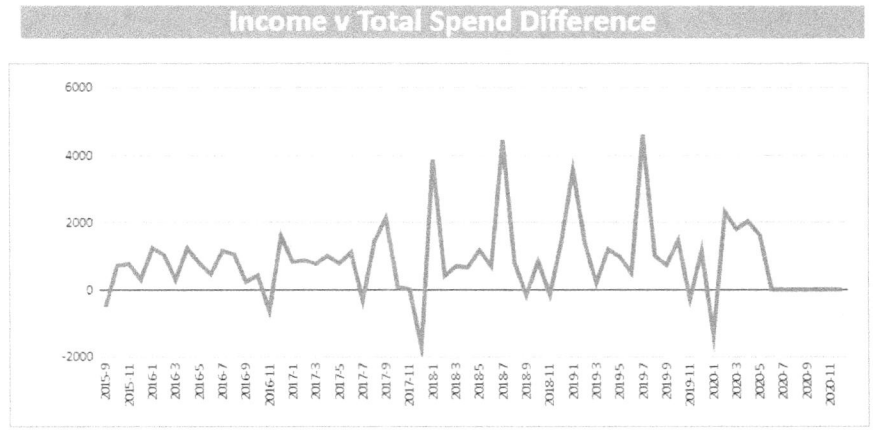

A graph on our dashboard showing that we generally underspend against our income each month

When we reached financial independence, we were at a 'tracking crossroads'. We could have switched to just keeping an eye on our HBS, which would alert us if our net worth started to drop. However, we decided to keep up the same level of HPL tracking that we've done for the past five years and we'll likely keep doing it for the foreseeable future. Not only is it very useful when it comes to retrieving all the details we need for self-assessment tax returns and accounts for our partnership business, but a great deal can (and in some ways should) change over a thirty or forty-year retirement. We still see our lives as a financial experiment. We can't be 100% sure whether we'll head off into the sunset at 65 laughing at the years of extra life we've given ourselves, or if we'll be living off baked beans and applying for jobs.

What we do know is that new work or entrepreneur opportunities and ideas can and will arise. Volunteer projects, learning opportunities, options to travel in new ways and meet people living different lives to us, are all out there, waiting for us. Tracking gifts us clarity over whether our crazy financial experiment is working.

In Summary

Attaining early financial independence has gifted us levels of freedom and control over our lives we couldn't even imagine a decade ago. It's enabled us to be ourselves, to think for ourselves, to travel or stay put as we want to. We no longer feel the stresses attached to maintaining an income needed to fund a high-consumption lifestyle which we don't need to be comfortable and happy. Life's good. It's not without its challenges, but these difficulties are solvable in a life where we have control and feel free to chart our own course.

And Finally

Getting financially independent is difficult, but it's not the impossible task it's often portrayed to be. Educate yourself, read about risk and fear, be introspective about your values and behaviours, start to take the action you need to take and slowly but surely the results will come. It's not a quick path, but it's a worthwhile one, and it can even be fun! The flexibility you'll gain, the ownership of your time, the self-determination of the non-trepreneur, are all out-of-this world once you hit the eventual goal.

The very best of luck to you,

Jason and Julie

Appendix A: Savings Ideas

" He who buys what he does not need, steals from himself."

Swedish Proverb

Writing about ideas for saving money is difficult without knowing who the audience is going to be. For someone earning minimum wage, these 'ideas' are going to be common-sense, and of little use. Their incomes won't allow them to spend more, unless they rely on credit to do so. For those on higher salaries though, the ideas may well look completely unworkable, or unpalatable at best.

My approach has been to include some cost-savings approaches for broad categories of spending simply to give some insight into the non-trepreneurial mindset. We use many of these strategies ourselves.

Transport

- Live within walking or cycling distance of work and schools, or at least minimise your commuting distance.
- Walk or cycle anything less than two miles in good weather.
- Own a single car.
- Buy second-hand cars, with a full-service history and at least 5 years old, avoiding the high depreciation in their early years of ownership.
- Use review sites to get the lowdown on reliability before buying a car, ignoring commonly held beliefs about the reliability of certain makes.
- Don't pay for finance or lease cars.
- Service cars according to the schedule (we get ours done yearly – but ideally service it yourself if you have the space).
- Buy discounted travel cards for public transport services.

Appendix A: Savings Ideas

- Avoid systematically paying for car parking (often there are free spaces a short walk away).
- Shop around for lower cost fuel, typically at your local supermarket.

Housing

- Learn DIY skills: decorating, tiling, fit flooring, self-assembling flat-pack furniture, plumbing, fitting shelves etc.
- Live within walking distance of a supermarket, gym, pubs, restaurants, library and public transport.
- Work from home when possible.
- Rent out your spare rooms or buy a house with only the bedroom(s) you need to sleep in.
- Look at second-hand furniture and appliances, they can often be much cheaper than new, even after hiring a van.
- Upgrade according to need, not fashion or status.
- Fit loft and cavity wall insulation (ideally with a government-backed discount).
- Do your own gardening, ironing, cleaning and so on.

Food

- Learn to cook!
- Treat eating and snacking out as a luxury, not a necessity.
- Avoid all food and drink vending machines.
- Treat low-cost supermarkets as a life-hack, not a fall in personal status.
- Compare similar items using the cost per kilogram or litre.
- Ignore convenience foods, like pre-packaged bowls of oats.
- Eat healthily (and exercise) to increase your quality of life, and as a side-effect reduce your need for health insurance.
- Switch to own shop brand or budget brand ranges.

Clothing
- Buy better quality, longer-lasting footwear and clothing.
- Avoid paying for branded clothing just to get the label.
- Buy second-hand from charity shops.
- Get last season's running shoes online at a big discount.

Pets
- Don't get a dog until you're able to stay at home and look after it yourself, avoiding paying for daytime boarding or walking.
- Self-insure pets, saving money when they're young and healthy to cover costs in later life.
- Do recurring maintenance yourself, like fur and claw cutting.
- Ignore over-priced specialist foods or treats.
- Check if medication is cheaper online, which it can be even accounting for the vet's prescription charge.

Entertainment
- Scale down your TV package, switch to Freeview or ditch the TV completely.
- Read up-to-date, quality magazines online for free from your library.
- Listen to music for free with ad-funded services like YouTube and Spotify.
- Buy used DVDs, CDs and books from charity shops.
- Join your local library for free books.

Holidays
- Compare package deals with booking direct or AirBnB and budget airlines.
- Take fewer, longer holidays. Much of the cost involved is getting you to and from your destination.
- If possible, go away outside of school holidays.

Appendix A: Savings Ideas

- Book as far in advance as you can, or if you can be flexible hold out for a last-minute deal.

Insurance
- Insure only what you can't afford to replace.
- Don't buy extended guarantees.
- Use cost comparison sites to find cheaper deals.
- Don't auto-renew each year, check for cheaper offers, no matter how painful the process!

Technology
- Buy according to need, not want or status.
- Buy refurbished or second hand.
- Learn to fix things like your smartphone.
- Shop around for low-cost SIM cards, only paying for all-you-can eat if you'll use a high volume of calls, texts or data.
- Use review websites to find the latest equipment at the lowest cost which meets your needs.
- When buying online do a search to see if there are any discount codes for the retailer and/or use a cashback site.
- Don't buy gadgets on a whim, avoid Amazon while under the influence!

Taxes
While these aren't quite money saving ideas, improving your knowledge about the tax system can save you money when it comes to making decisions about where to invest.

- Invest inside ISAs.
- Learn how income tax is calculated.
- Learn the tax rules around pensions and buy-to-let.
- Complete your own self-assessment tax returns, taking advice from an accountant where necessary.
- Use a specialist for complex tax questions.

Appendix B: Further Support

"If I have seen further, it is by standing on the shoulders of giants."

Sir Isaac Newton, English Mathematician, Physicist, Astronomer, Theologian and Author

There are a broad range of resources available to help with your personal push towards financial independence. These books, blogs and other resources are often available for free or for a low cost and are pure gold in terms of accelerating your own path to freedom. Every penny and minute spent reading, watching or listening to this information is money and time very well used.

Books

This is a selection of the personal finance books I've read and can highly recommend:

- The *Meaningful Money Handbook* by Pete Matthew
- *Your Money or Your Life* by Vicki Robin (get the 2008 version)
- *The Financial Times Guide to Investing* by Glen Arnold
- *Master the Money Game* by Tony Robbins
- *The Simple Path to Wealth* by J L Collins
- *The Intelligent Investor* by Benjamin Graham
- *The Millionaire Next Door* by Thomas J. Stanley and William D. Danko
- *The Richest Man in Babylon* by George S Clayson
- *How to Own the World* by Andrew Craig
- *Rich Dad Poor Dad* by Robert Kiyosaki and Sharon Lechter

Appendix B: Further Support

Websites and Blogs

There are thousands of personal finance websites and blogs out there these days. The following is a selection of the ones I've found to be most authoritative, entertaining and educational.

- **Meaningful Money** (*meaningfulmoney.tv*). Pete Matthew is a chartered financial planner and has built up an enormous wealth of plain English blog posts, videos and podcasts which describe a broad range of personal finance topics for the layman. If you're not quite sure what a pension, stock or an ISA is, this is a great place to spend a while learning the basics (and the more advanced topics too).
- **Investopedia** (*investopedia.com*). This website does a great job of describing and demystifying the terminology used in the world of finance.
- **Early Retirement Extreme** (*earlyretirementextreme.com*). Jacob Lund Fisker is perhaps the original FIRE blogger, describing his focus on consumerism, frugality, investing and living a good life. His blog is huge, but he's condensed his thoughts into a book of the same name, if you want the best stuff all in one place.
- **Mr Money Mustache** (*www.mrmoneymustache.com*). Probably the most famous of the FIRE blogs, it's no longer updated frequently by the author Pete Adeney, but the array of posts it contains are classics, written in a punchy, entertaining style.
- **The Escape Artist** (*theescapeartist.me*). The most established UK FIRE blog, written by ex-accountant Barney Whiter. Discusses similar concepts to other FIRE blogs, but from a British perspective.
- **Monevator** (*monevator.com*). Written by two UK-based anonymous bloggers and provides motivational, educational and entertaining posts on various aspects of personal finance and investing.

- **Jlcollinsnh** (*jlcollinsnh.com*). Authored by J L Collins, the main attraction of this blog for me is the focus on using index tracker funds to build wealth. The author has also distilled his thoughts into a book, *The Simple Path to Wealth*, which I highly recommend reading.

Podcasts

I can't honestly say I've ever managed to get into listening to podcasts, but I come across them from time to time and have pulled together a short list below to get you started in case this format works for you:

- *meaningfulmoney.tv/mmpodcast*
- *www.radicalpersonalfinance.com*
- *www.financialwell-being.co.uk*
- *propertyhub.net*
- *www.moneytothemasses.com*
- *firedrillpodcast.com*

US Translator

Most of the financial independence blogs, books and websites are published in the USA. They refer to terms which won't be familiar to a UK-based non-trepreneur. There's a brief translation below to help UK readers of US-published material.

- **401(k)** – an employer-provided pension, like a defined-contribution occupational pension in the UK.
- **IRA (Individual Retirement Account)** – like a UK ISA but money can't usually be withdrawn before age 59½ from an IRA without paying a penalty.
- **Social Security** – a similar concept to the UK state pension.
- **Health Care** – there is no universal free-to-use national health service in the USA, so health insurance is a much more important and discussed topic in US-based media.

Appendix B: Further Support

- **S&P 500** – the Standard and Poor's index of 500 of the largest companies in the US, a rough equivalent to the FTSE 100 in the UK but obviously with more companies!
- **IRS (Inland Revenue Service)** – the US equivalent of the HMRC tax collection service in the UK.
- **Tax Returns** – in the UK anyone with only PAYE income doesn't need to complete a tax return. In the US most employees must file a tax return each year.

About the Authors

Julie and Jason Buckley quit work just before they turned 40 in 2011, to take a once in a lifetime, one-year tour of Europe in their motorhome. Documenting their travels on their blog *ourtour.co.uk*, two years later they finally returned home. Yearning for more adventures, they set a goal to change their lives and become financially free, enabling them to travel whenever they wanted to.

Aged 43, they 'retired' and took to the road once more to explore from the North Cape in Norway to the Sahara Desert in Morocco. They now mix up their time between motorhome life and their base in Nottinghamshire, England. Julie and Jason have written several books to help and inspire others to follow their own motorhome dreams or to start their own journey to financial freedom.

When not travelling, Julie and Jason live in a small town outside Nottingham in the UK. To get in touch, or follow future travels, any of these will work:

- **Email**: julieandjason@ourtour.co.uk
- **Web**: *ourtour.co.uk*
- **Youtube**: search *youtube.com* for 'ourtour blog'
- **Instagram**: *www.instagram.com/ourtourblog*
- **Twitter**: @ourtourblog
- **Facebook**: search *facebook.com* for 'ourtour blog'

A Cheeky Request

Thank you for buying and reading our book, we really appreciate it and hope it inspires you to think a bit differently about money.

If you have enjoyed the book or found it useful, please take a moment to leave us a review on Amazon. These really help other readers and give us feedback too on how we can improve later editions.

About the Authors

Other Books by the Authors

In addition to their blog, Julie and Jason have written and published several books, all available through Amazon:

- **Funding Freedom** – the forerunner to this book. A free mini-guide to financial freedom, explaining how they set up their lifestyle and finances to enable long-term travel in their early 40s.
- **The 200** – Showcasing 200 of the most memorable, inspirational and interesting places we've stayed, in over a decade of motorhome touring.
- **Motorhome Touring Handbook** – Packed full of practical advice from choosing a motorhome and touring the UK to travelling abroad or planning for and enjoying a year-long tour.
- **Motorhome France** – all the practical info you need to take your motorhome to the most visited country in the World.
- **Motorhome Morocco** – The book we wanted to buy before our first trip to Morocco! It guides you through the process of planning and enjoying a tour of this incredible North African country.
- **A Monkey Ate My Breakfast** – A travelogue of our first motorhome tour of Morocco in 2011, an eye-opening adventure onto a new continent, and into a new and exotic culture.
- **OurTour Downloaded** – All the blog posts from our first year of full-time motorhome touring, handily gathered into one ebook.

www.ingramcontent.com/pod-product-compliance
Lightning Source LLC
Chambersburg PA
CBHW060835220526
45466CB00003B/1119